130 FAQs
and Practical Answers
from Scholastic's Teacher Helpline

Ruth Manna

NEW YORK • TORONTO • LONDON • AUCKLAND • SYDNEY
MEXICO CITY • NEW DELHI • HONG KONG • BUENOS AIRES

Teaching
Resources

To my children, Mario, Dante, and Julia, and my many students.
You shaped me more than I shaped you.

Throughout this book you'll find Web site suggestions to support various activities. Please keep in mind that Internet locations and content can change over time. Always check Web sites in advance to make certain the intended information is still available and appropriate for your students.

Editor: Mela Ottaiano
Cover design by Jason Robinson
Interior design by Melinda Belter

ISBN-13: 978-0-545-10569-9
ISBN-10: 0-545-10569-2

2 3 4 5 6 7 8 9 10   40   15 14 13 12 11 10 09

CONTENTS

CHAPTER III. MANAGING A CLASSROOM

Routine Classroom Management

Handling Difficult Situations

CHAPTER IV. ASSESSING STUDENT PROGRESS

CHAPTER V. PLANNING CURRICULUM

Reading

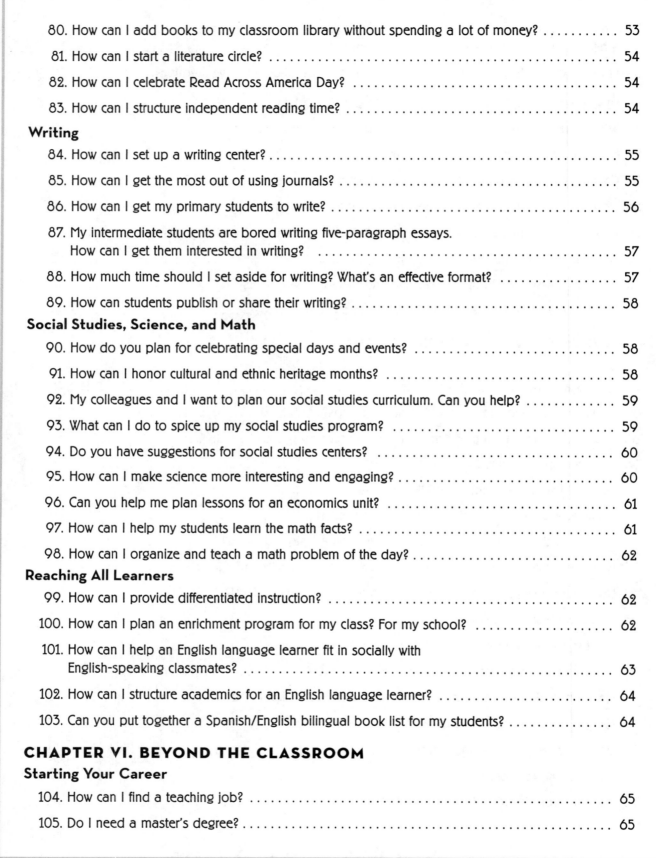

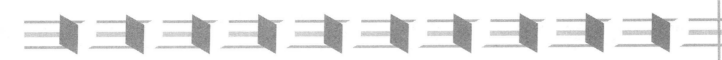

INTRODUCTION

I start every school year with butterflies in my stomach and the anticipation of a beginner. After many years as a teacher, I'm still filled with the hope a new year brings. Learning to teach has been a process of trial and error, refining skills with years of practice. Daily reflection has made me adjust my teaching. As I've gained skill, I've learned to trust myself—and my intuition. But I still have questions and problems.

If you're like me, you want down-to-earth responses to everyday problems from a trusted source. Because teaching can be isolating, we may not always have a colleague to answer our questions. And with the demands of the job, we may not have time to ask. I hope this book of practical answers will address your day-to-day questions.

What's the story behind this book?

In 2005 the staff of Scholastic Inc. and I had the idea that teachers would pose questions to a message board if they knew that a veteran teacher would respond. Since I'd already been an online mentor teacher at www.scholastic.com, I volunteered to take on the project, and the New Teacher Helpline began. I agreed to answer each question personally, consulting with colleagues, Web sites, and books as needed.

"How do you find time?" my colleagues often ask. Whenever I have a minute I respond, usually late at night or early in the morning. Gradually, I've developed a voice that is equal parts patient colleague, encouraging mom, and enthusiastic cheerleader.

By early 2009, there were nearly 2,000 posts on the helpline. So teachers can more readily utilize the wealth of information in the archive, I have gathered the most frequently asked questions (FAQs) and responses in this book. The table of contents, with numbered questions and organized by key topics, makes it easy to find needed information.

Teachers ask a broad variety of questions, ranging from organization and classroom management to curriculum planning and communicating with parents. Just when I think I've heard it all, a teacher surprises me with a new question.

Who is this book for?

130 FAQs and Practical Answers From Scholastic's Teacher Helpline is for all teachers of elementary school (K–6)—new and veteran—seeking practical solutions to everyday situations. While this book will answer many of your questions, if you have one that isn't addressed here, you can still post it and receive a reassuring response!

Best wishes to you!
Ruth Manna
Conway, Massachusetts
March 2009

You can reach me with your questions at Scholastic's Teacher Helpline:
http://community.scholastic.com/scholastic/board?board.id=emergency

---

Here are my top three Web sites for all teachers, grades K–6:

Scholastic.com

http://www.scholastic.com A site for teachers, administrators, librarians, students, and parents. Rich and deep with lessons, printables, interactive activities and games, author chats, social networks for teachers, and other resources, scholastic.com has so much to offer.

Pete MacKay's Teacher List

http://www.theteacherlist.ca Edmonton, Alberta, teacher and technology expert, Pete MacKay will send you a Web site a day if you join his listserv. Teachers refer sites to Pete who vets them prior to recommending them. There is an

archive of sites featured from 2001 to the present. This site is a must!

Edutopia and the George Lucas Educational Foundation

http://www.edutopia.org George Lucas' (Star Wars) Educational Foundation has an educator's Web site devoted to technology and professional development. *Edutopia* is a magazine that comes in both hard-copy and online formats. There are weekly e-newsletters about technology and project learning, information about grants, education news, etc.

PLANNING FOR A NEW SCHOOL YEAR

1. What can I do to prepare over the summer?

If you are a new teacher, congratulations! Summer is a great time to plan because there are fewer distractions. No one's interrupting you midsentence asking you to tie her shoe. Below are several ways new and returning teachers can prepare now for the beginning of school.

Classroom: If you have access to your classroom, look through closets and cupboards and decide what you want to keep. Consider your curriculum, but also what makes sense. Less really is more because the less you have, the easier it will be to organize.

As you spend time in your classroom, your room will become a source of inspiration. Arrange your furniture in a variety of ways. Consider getting rid of furniture that's not essential. Measure your bulletin boards and decide how you will use them. Organize your class library by topic and reading level. Make a wish list of items you'd like for your room.

Long-range planning: Even if you can't get into to your classroom, there's a lot you can do at home. Get a copy of state standards or frameworks on your state's department of education Web site. If you have prescribed district or school curricula, get copies of those as well. You will need these documents along with textbooks as you plan. Talk with a coteacher or mentor to get input before you put time into creating a plan.

Libraries, Web sites, and bookstores: Once you have a long-range plan, gather books and materials to correlate with units you'll teach. Visit public libraries in your area or use an interlibrary loan to get appropriate books on a range of reading levels. Read books to prepare for reading instruction, read-alouds, and literature circles. Search for Web sites and download materials you think you'll use with your students. Make note of online games and activities. Visit local or online bookstores and compile a bibliography of books to support your curriculum. You may want to search online first, then stop by a bookstore to skim books before buying.

Lists and forms: If you have a copy of your class list, you can make lists and forms. It may be helpful to have two class lists, one arranged alphabetically by first name and the other by last name. Print name labels for double-pocket folders and print calendars, certificates, and awards for your students. The more you do now, the less you'll have to do during the first weeks of school.

Welcome letter to students and parents: A few weeks before school starts, write a welcome letter to your students and their parents. Ask a school secretary for a list of names and addresses.

Tell families you're looking forward to meeting them. Include items you want students to remember on the first day of school. Add information about start time, bus schedules, or lunch money, anything to inform families and make them comfortable on the first day. I usually ask students to bring a book they have read and feel confident reading, which gives me an idea of their reading level. In addition, if you take a vacation, send your new students a postcard from your destination.

Welcome party: Some schools have an ice cream social or potluck supper to welcome new teachers. Check with your principal or mentor teacher.

2. Should I contact my coteachers and my mentor this summer?

It is a thoughtful, polite gesture to call or e-mail coteachers and your mentor to introduce yourself. Keep conversations or notes brief and light. Your colleagues may be focused on summer jobs or their children's activities, but they will be pleased you contacted them.

If a colleague offers to meet you for lunch or coffee, accept the invitation. Bring a list of questions to your get-together so you can have your questions answered without taking too much of the other person's time.

At the end of the summer, you will likely meet colleagues while you work in your room preparing for school. If no one approaches you, take the initiative to visit other teachers, introduce yourself, and compliment them on their classrooms. During these visits you may have more opportunities to ask questions.

Classroom Organization

3. How can I de-clutter my classroom?

If you are a new teacher or a teacher who is moving to a new classroom, look carefully at your furniture and consider how you'll use your room. You may decide to eliminate several pieces of furniture. Just what do you need? In addition to desks or tables and chairs for each student, you'll want:

- table and chairs for meeting with small groups
- open space where your entire class can gather
- area rug
- table and chairs for an assistant or special educator
- computer station
- listening center
- study carrels or "offices" around the perimeter of the room
- supplies and storage unit accessible to students
- classroom library with floor pillows or beanbag chairs
- milk crates (or small stools) with clipboards for working away from desks
- overhead/LED projector, laptop stand, and easel

> There's a wonderful article, "The Difference Is Amazing," by Gayle Robert, an experienced teacher who decided to de-clutter her classroom. Her de-cluttered room had a positive impact on her students' ability to focus and learn. It appeared in Spring 2001 edition of the *Responsive Classroom Newsletter*—found on the Responsive Classroom/Northeast Foundation for Children, Inc. (NEFC) Web site: http://www.responsiveclassroom.org/pdf_files/13_2nl_3.pdf

Once you understand what your curriculum is, skim books and teaching materials. (If you are taking over a classroom, you may find a previous teacher's materials have little meaning for you.) Keep teacher resources you will use and literature on a range of reading levels. You'll add your own books and teacher resources as time and money permit. The less you have, the easier it will be to keep your room neat and well-organized.

About ten days before school starts, organize school supplies so students can get them independently. Set up a class library or bookshelf featuring books that tie in with your first units of study. Distribute texts and workbooks. Organize double pocket folders color-coded by subject. Label

desks and chairs with students' names. Plan and assemble bulletin boards and door decorations. When students enter a classroom that is set up, they can begin learning right away and you can capitalize on their initial excitement.

4. What supplies will I need?

So much depends on school policy, curriculum, and grade level. Some schools pay for all classroom supplies. In other schools, teachers or parents purchase supplies. Talk this over with your principal and colleagues before you make purchases.

The following items are supplies typically needed in an elementary school classroom:

glue sticks	homework folders	copy paper
bottles of school glue	double-pocket colored folders	card stock
tacky glue	watercolor markers	lined paper
scissors	boxes of watercolors	graph paper
rulers	tempera paints	bulletin board paper
meter sticks and yardsticks	paintbrushes	decorative bulletin board trim
math manipulatives (rods, cubes, tangrams, number lines, 100 chart, etc.)	chalk	stapler and staples
	whiteboards	index cards
crayons	dry erase markers (whiteboard)	sentence strips
colored pencils	wet erase markers (overhead)	poster board
#2 pencils	transparencies for overhead	wet wipes
erasers	colored sidewalk chalk	band-aids
staple remover	Cray-Pas	tissues
push pins or thumbtacks	black Flair pens	stopwatch
rubber bands	black Sharpies	stickers
resealable plastic bags	highlighters	other art supplies (pipe cleaners, glitter, etc.)
brads/paper fasteners	colored construction paper	

5. I'm on a tight budget. How can I get the supplies I need?

Here are several sources for supplies:

Classroom allowance: Check with your principal because she may have budgeted funds for each classroom for supplies.

Parent-Teacher Organization: In many schools, the PTO makes a small donation to each teacher in September. Check with your administrator or PTO.

Parents: In your welcome letter to parents and students, include an optional list of supplies each student might bring on the first day. Not all families can afford to purchase supplies, so mention it's a suggested list. Check with an administrator or coworker first. Office supply stores have grade-specific supply lists that give parents an idea about items families typically purchase.

Wish list: Your school may encourage teachers to make wish lists that are posted online or handed out on Back-to-School Night. Select a wide price range of items, from pencils and glue sticks to board games and DVDs.

Garage sales, friends, and family: Garage sales are typically a great source for games and children's books. Your relatives and friends with grown-up children may have slightly used books and toys they'd be willing to donate.

Recycling center: At my town dump we have a swap shop. Residents drop off items they no longer need and others are free to take them. This is a fun activity for a Saturday morning.

Discount and dollar stores: Discount and dollar stores have excellent prices on school supplies, though quality varies and not everything is a bargain. Begin checking school supplies aisles in July because the best items are snapped up quickly. I've found sturdy plastic homework folders and Crayola markers, among other bargains.

Office supply store: My local office supply store has Teacher Appreciation Day in August. There are freebies, coupons, and sale items.

6. How will I set up my classroom desks?

How you arrange the desks depends on several factors:

- number and age of students
- size of classroom
- amount of storage space
- school policies and practices

There are many attractive ways to arrange desks. For older students who do small-group work, pushing together tables or desks to form larger tables makes sense.

Another idea is to have students sit next to just one partner. Pairing students with different strengths works well.

If you anticipate that discipline will be challenging, start with students in rows facing forward. This arrangement is an effective way to maintain control.

I like to place students' desks in a U shape facing the front of the room. This arrangement allows students to see one another and me and promotes a feeling of community. The open middle of the room, defined by an area rug, is a gathering place for the whole class. On opposite sides of the room are a table for reading groups and a second table for my classroom assistant. Four quiet "offices" for individuals are scattered around the room. Listening center, supplies center, library, pet area, and games shelf are around the outside of the room.

Set aside several days at the end of the summer to work in your classroom and experiment with a variety of desk arrangements.

7. What extras can I add to make my room special?

Think creatively! Special touches make your classroom distinctive. Add one or two extras at a time. Try some of these ideas:

Barstool: You can see students seated in the back of the room when you are perched on a barstool, a great spot for read-alouds.

Rocking chair: A rocking chair near an area rug is a nice place for you to sit during Morning Meeting. Two young students can buddy-read in a rocker.

Folding floor chairs: I found padded folding chairs at a discount store for $10. They are similar to beach chairs. Students take turns sharing six chairs.

Posters: A bookstore might donate posters. Check the American Library Association, too. They have colorful, inexpensive posters.

Magnets: Brightly colored magnets work on both whiteboards and blackboards.

Ceiling clips: Clips or hooks available at a teacher store make it easy to hang artwork from a suspended ceiling.

Clothesline: A clothesline can be used for drying and displaying paintings.

Caddies: Small plastic caddies for pens and pencils work well on tables.

8. Can you suggest bins, baskets, and organizers for my classroom?

Plastic bins and baskets in a variety of sizes and colors work well. Although teacher stores sell these items, you may find less expensive, sturdy ones at discount or office supply stores. Be sure baskets are strong enough to hold books. The kinds of baskets and bins you may need include:

- large baskets for completed work and homework folders
- clear plastic storage containers with lids for supplies and toys
- individual small bins or "tool kits" for frequently used supplies

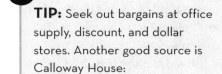

TIP: Seek out bargains at office supply, discount, and dollar stores. Another good source is Calloway House: http://www.callowayhouse.com

- supply caddies for the center of tables
- milk crates for clipboards
- portable file folder box for work samples and assessments
- small plastic filing cabinet on wheels for teaching materials
- cardboard book boxes for individuals and for storing books by topic or reading level

In addition to baskets, you may want five color-coded folders for teacher resources and plans, one for each day of the week.

Organizers are expensive, so buy a few at a time and add them to your wish list.

9. My classroom is an actual storage closet. How can I make it homey?

A special educator once asked me what to do about her classroom, a windowless storage closet. She wanted to make it an appealing, cozy room for her nine students. Her room was crowded with furniture, which was contributing to behavior problems and loss of morale. Here were my suggestions:

- Remove most of the furniture, including the teacher's desk, and replace it with one round table and chairs.
- Push a second small table against the wall. Keep the middle of the room open.
- Use table and floor lamps for more light.

- Mount shelves on the walls to save floor space.
- Add an area rug.
- Create a book nook in a corner with beanbag chairs, floor pillows, and rug.
- With students' help, paint a large mural of an open window looking out onto a beautiful landscape.
- Glue carpet squares or Styrofoam to ductwork to cushion sound.

Lesson Plans

10. How should I begin planning?

Gather textbooks, teachers' manuals, state standards or frameworks, and district and school curricula. If your students will be assessed by statewide tests, it is important that you teach to state standards. Teaching to standards is not teaching to a test.

If your school or district has its own curricula, you will need to be in sync with that. Look for concepts and skills that your state, district, and school have in common.

Make copies of standards and curriculum guides and put them into three-ring binders. Next, read classroom textbooks while thinking about state standards. Some texts teach beyond state standards, so you may not need to teach an entire text. Prioritize, allowing time to first teach what you must. For example, my second graders are responsible for learning addition and subtraction with regrouping and math facts with sums to 20, so I spend a lot of time on those aspects of math. I don't teach multiplication, although multiplication is in my text, but I do teach skip counting, part of learning to multiply.

Read student texts and workbooks first, because you want to know what students will read. Directions may be tricky and concepts may be difficult, so take notes as you read.

Then skim the teachers' manuals. Get the big picture and don't worry about the details. Look for pacing guidelines.

Using a large (18" x 24") academic-year desk calendar and packets of sticky notes or index cards, map out the year. Begin by recording holidays, professional development days and vacations. Next, select units that address state standards. Then, write the units or chapter headings on sticky notes and move them around on the calendar. Ideally, you want units and read-aloud chapter books to end before vacations because students lose interest and forget over a break. If a unit has two or three big questions or overarching concepts, make sure you set aside enough time and teach them using more than one modality. Finally, move around the notes until you have covered the curriculum and are happy with the flow.

A yearlong guide is a sketch that will be revised as a school year progresses. Each class is unique, and your pace is influenced by the time it takes students to master concepts and skills.

11. Is there an accepted lesson plan form?

There is more than one accepted way to write a lesson plan. Check with colleagues so you will use the format your principal prefers. Here is one accepted lesson format:

Objectives: Purpose of lesson stated as behaviors students will exhibit

Materials: Items you and your students will need to complete lesson

Set up and preparation: Things to do ahead of time

Procedures: Step-by-step directions, including mini-lesson, discussion questions, and activity

Assessment: What did students learn? What methods will you use to check their understanding?

Supporting all learners: Accommodations for diverse learners

Assignments: Follow-up activity or homework assignment

Home connection: Parent communication

Evaluation: Self-reflection about lesson, what you'll do differently next time

12. How can I turn state standards into a year of lessons?

State standards will tell you what typical students are expected to learn in a given grade. Read standards for your grade as well as one grade above and below it, so you will understand the grade-to-grade progression. Some students will be on grade level while others will be above or below grade level. Standards differ from state to state. The more specific the standards, the easier it will be to teach them.

Standards are a guide. The substance of your curriculum is usually established at a district or school level. Be sure to read district and school curricula and look for areas of similarity among state, district, and school.

Use highlighters in a variety of colors. As you read student texts or teacher's manuals, highlight the concepts and skills that are covered by state standards. Then start planning.

13. Can you help me develop a pacing plan?

Appropriate pacing is a tricky skill for teachers to develop. In part, this is because we are frequently asked to teach more than we can possibly accomplish in one school year. Pacing is also challenging because it varies from year to year based on students' readiness and motivation.

There is a tendency to proceed slowly so every student masters a given skill before moving ahead. Depending upon the make-up of your class, this may or may not be realistic.

It helps to know state standards, units of study, and key concepts before beginning a school year. It's also beneficial to have an overview of the curriculum along with a yearlong plan. For a new teacher, working with a mentor teacher or colleague is also a good idea.

To keep on-track, move through daily lessons toward a culminating activity. Before starting a social studies or

TIP: To force you to complete a unit, publicly announce a culminating activity. For example, tell students several weeks in advance that an International Luncheon to celebrate the end of your Immigration unit will take place on a given date. Your announcement will push you toward the end of the unit.

science unit, plan a culminating activity, like a panel discussion, art project, or field trip. In math, a culminating activity could be a chapter test followed by a discussion and reteaching a concept. Ask yourself at the end of every day, "Have I advanced the curriculum today?"

At the end of each unit, it's important to reread your yearlong plan. You may need to make adjustments in pacing in order to teach everything you have planned.

14. What is the difference between a skill and a concept?

A skill is a discrete bit of knowledge acquired through training and practice. An example of a skill is, "Student will skip count by five to one hundred."

Students learn to skip count with manipulatives, a number line, and a 100 chart. At first, young children may skip count by rote. Students understand number patterns more deeply as their thinking matures.

A concept is an abstract thought. When a student is able to put bits of knowledge together and construct meaning, then he conceptualizes. A student who understands a concept is able to generalize and apply his knowledge to different situations.

A student who understands the concept of number patterns doesn't need to begin with the number five to skip count by five. He may also apply skip counting to multiplication and division.

15. When and how do teachers use themes?

School-wide themes: Schools may have school-wide themes that last from several months to an entire academic year. For example, a school may feature "Honesty" one month and "Sharing" the next. Or a whole school may study Mexican history and culture for an academic year.

Grades K–2: Primary grade teachers often teach with themes. A teacher who uses this approach puts all subjects under a thematic umbrella. Planning thematically is challenging because finding materials across all subject areas is time-consuming. Themes usually change weekly, monthly, or bimonthly. The older the students, the longer they can sustain interest in a theme.

Grades 3–6: Teachers in grades 3–6 typically teach by units of study rather than themes. They may teach an American Revolution history unit concurrently with a literature unit on Greek myths and a science unit about simple machines.

CHAPTER II

BEGINNING THE SCHOOL YEAR

16. What does a typical school day look like?

A typical school day in an elementary school revolves around literacy. All activities become opportunities to teach reading and writing. Since students are expected to read and write across the curriculum, literacy lessons extend to math, science, and social studies. In grades K–2 the emphasis is on basic skills in reading and math. In grades 3–6, in addition to language arts and math, students spend time studying science, technology, and social studies. Younger students are learning to read while older students use their reading skills to learn.

Usually students are with one classroom teacher, which facilitates building strong relationships with students and parents. This teacher creates an orderly atmosphere of calm acceptance in which students can relax and take risks as learners.

There is a balance of opposites in an elementary classroom:

Talking and listening: Effective teachers talk less than half the time. To encourage participation, you'll want to ask follow-up questions and reinterpret responses for a group.

"Were you saying . . .?"

"I thought I heard you say . . ."

To encourage divergent thinking, elicit multiple responses to questions. In math, if there is one correct answer, share strategies.

"What equation did you use?"

"Did anyone use a different equation?"

"Tell me what you were thinking as you solved this problem."

Moving and sitting still: It's important to have legitimate opportunities for students to move around. They could read in a book nook, do morning exercises, or play an active game. We do Brain Gym exercises every day before we practice handwriting. Students write better when they move around first.

> *The First Six Weeks of School,* by Paula Denton and Roxanne Kriete (NEFC, 2000), has a lot of helpful information.

Noise and quiet: There is time for yelling during wild activity and for quiet while students read silently. There's a healthy buzz, an ideal volume, when students are fully engaged in a task.

Left brain and right brain: You'll want to have activities for students who are intuitive and creative as well as those who think logically and strategically.

Intense concentration and relaxation: School is hard work, but save time for fun and relaxation. Celebrating cultures and holidays with songs, stories, and art enriches students' lives. My class loves April Fool's Day because we play tricks on other classes. On Martin Luther King, Jr.'s birthday, we celebrate with a birthday cake.

17. How can I have a smooth start to my school year?

Leadership: Teachers build relationships with students, but as the leader, keep a professional distance between you and your students. It's tempting to think you can be both children's leader and friend, but you can't. Believe it or not, students want you to lead.

It's equally important to accept all students and treat them fairly. Though you may like some students more than others you cannot show favoritism. In part, this is for your protection, and to do otherwise is unethical.

Organization: Arrange your books and materials logically. Make sure student desks and supply cabinets are well organized. Put away items you are not using to avoid clutter. Have your plan book open and keep your eye on the clock as you progress through the day.

Room set-up: Spend a week before school opens setting up your classroom and putting materials on students' desks so you can begin teaching on the first day.

Planning: In the beginning, avoid downtime by planning well. Have a list of additional activities in case students complete their assignments. As the year progresses, they will learn to use free time wisely.

Set boundaries with parents: Welcome parents warmly without getting into long conversations. Let them know you're looking forward to meeting them at Back-to-School Night. Suggest they write you a note or make an appointment if they have an issue. It's your job to teach their children, and you need to be available primarily to students before and during the day.

Morning Meeting: Morning Meeting is a daily activity that sets a positive tone for the day. Students may recite the Pledge of Allegiance and their class promise. There may be announcements, sharing, and a short read-aloud. Sit in a circle so all can see.

Rules: Clear, simple rules are best. A list of five rules works well. Be sure to have a copy of your class rules posted on chart paper. Send parents the rules so they will know what to expect and support you.

Keep it simple: Remember that the school year is new for everyone, including you. Have realistic, modest expectations, knowing you will increase your expectations once students are relaxed and comfortable.

18. What will I need to remember for the first day?

Good night's sleep: Though you may have trouble falling asleep, try to get a good night's rest. Get up two hours before you plan to leave for school so you won't have to rush. Eat a nutritious breakfast.

Snack and lunch: Bring a healthful snack and lunch. Drink plenty of water.

Bright colors: Elementary students respond to bright colors. If you wear a colorful shirt or crazy socks or tie/scarf, it will help you hold your students' attention.

Bring flowers: A vase of fresh flowers makes your room welcoming.

Arrive early: Plan to arrive at least one hour before school begins. Parents typically bring students on the first day and many students arrive early.

Check in with coteachers: Stop by your colleagues' classrooms to wish them well.

Small goodie bags: Set up paper lunch bags with a colorful pencil, eraser, granola bar, and bookmark to welcome students. If providing a treat, check for food allergies first.

Stay calm: The more calm you appear, the more easily students will settle down. Students take their cues from you.

19. Can you suggest poems and picture books for the first day of school?

Poems

Thanks to Tim Rasinski for the first three poetry suggestions:

"Al Veevo, Al Vivo . . ." (School Cheer)

"Good Books, Good Times" by Lee Bennett Hopkins

"Invitation" by Shel Silverstein

"Children, Children Everywhere!" by Jack Prelutsky

Almost Late for School: And More School Poems by Carol Shields and
    Paul Meisel

Picture Books

GRADES K–2

Chrysanthemum by Kevin Henkes

Enemy Pie by Derek Munson

How to Be a Friend: A Guide to Making Friends and Keeping Them by
    Laurie Krasny Brown and Marc Brown

The Kissing Hand by Audrey Penn

Yo! Yes? by Chris Raschka

Timothy Goes to School by Rosemary Wells

GRADES 3–6

A Friendship for Today by Patricia McKissack

That Dreadful Day by James Stevenson

A Walk in the Rain With a Brain by Edward M. Hallowell

20. What can I expect of my students on the first day of school?

Expect students to be on their best behavior and very excited on the first day of school. They will be more relaxed and natural on the second day and by the end of the first week, you'll begin to see who they really are.

Keep the first day light, with plenty of movement breaks and frequent changes in subjects or activities. This will help ease students' transition from an unstructured summer to a structured classroom. While you may discuss class rules, don't expect students to remember the details because they are just too nervous.

Students want to share their summer experiences with you and their classmates. Maybe they could make a graph of their summer activities. Or they might interview one another and share what they find out. If you give students a list of interview questions, it will help them focus.

21. Will you share your class promise with me?

Here's my class promise, with thanks to Debbie Miller, author of *Reading With Meaning* (Stenhouse, 2002).

Our Promise to Each Other

We care about each other and our classroom so we share what we have, speak kindly, listen carefully, help others learn, work hard, and include everyone. We know that everyone makes mistakes. We stand up for what is right, for ourselves and others. We take care of our classroom. We laugh and have fun!

We will keep our promise even when grown-ups aren't looking.

I copy our promise onto chart paper, and we all sign it on the first day of school. It is posted where the class can see it. We recite our promise at Morning Meeting right after the Pledge of Allegiance. Early in the year we discuss our promise and later refer to it when students break it. On Constitution Day, September 17th, we discuss our promise as a class constitution.

By midyear we recite our promise from memory. We make a circle, criss-cross our arms, and join hands. After the promise, we pass a hand squeeze around the circle and end by greeting one another with "Buenos Dias!"

Rituals like a class promise build community, reinforce prosocial values, and make students feel secure.

22. What rules will my students need?

Rules set necessary boundaries intended to foster mutual respect and prevent chaos. Respect for self, school community, and property is an all-inclusive rule. Review the concept of respect by giving concrete examples and asking students to role-play specific situations, both positive and negative.

Rules might include how to listen when a teacher is talking, what to do if two adults are talking, or what a student should do if he needs to leave the classroom.

A list of five rules is usually enough. Too many rules all at once can overwhelm students. When students have mastered five rules, you can add one or two additional rules as needed.

Check with colleagues and administrators before posting your class rules to make sure your expectations are consistent with those of your colleagues. There is a complete presentation of listening rules, like "Give Me Five," in Harry Wong's *The First Days of School* (Harry K. Wong Publications, Inc., 2004).

Think through logical consequences of broken rules. When rules are broken, be prepared to follow through consistently with consequences.

Send parents a copy of your class rules so they can support you at home.

23. How long will it take for my students to learn the rules?

The length of time it takes for students to learn rules depends on their ages.

Grades K–2: Younger students need between four to six weeks to learn rules, procedures, and expectations. They are learning to adapt to a school setting with specific rules so they need frequent reminders.

Grades 3–6: By this age, students have been in school several years, so it takes only two to three weeks to learn their new teacher's rules. The first time a student breaks a rule, you may want to give a warning, but let that student know there will be consequences next time.

24. What rules will I need for a computer center?

Most schools have an Internet Acceptable Use Policy to prevent improper use of the Internet, as well as filters to keep out inappropriate Web sites.

Consider implementing these rules for a computer center:

Hands off mouse: When you say, "Hands in your lap," students take their hands off the mouse to listen to directions.

Sharing: If two or three students share one computer, they need to take turns controlling the mouse.

Visiting Web sites: Students need to stay on the Web site their teacher has selected for them.

Whispering: Unless everyone has a computer with a headset, there will likely be talking, but you can insist on whispering.

Caring for headsets and software: Students should know how to use and put away headsets and software.

Printing: Students should ask before printing photos or documents.

25. I will miss the first week of school. What should my substitute do?

Grades K–2: A substitute can teach students classroom basics like how to make a circle or line up. In kindergarten, she might teach students to wash their hands and cough into their elbows. In addition to learning rules and expectations, second graders could visit the school library or media center. You will likely reteach these rules and routines when you return the following week.

Grades 3–6: A substitute could begin teaching a science or social studies unit. She could discuss summer reading with students and give them opportunities to share books they read recently. I would not ask a substitute to do formal assessments.

26. How can I incorporate diversity into my classroom?

Acceptance of diversity is an everyday occurrence in a classroom. Teaching students of different races, ethnicities, genders, religions, and socioeconomic classes means diversity is always on our minds. The time for teaching diversity is every day, not just during Hispanic Heritage Month or on Martin Luther King, Jr.'s birthday. To emphasize inclusion, you'll want your classroom to reflect many cultures in books, posters, and projects.

Here are several ways to teach diversity:

Literature and the arts: Books in our classroom libraries need to represent the many groups that make up the United States. Keep this in mind when selecting books for read-alouds or reading groups.

Through music and visual arts students, learn about those who are different from them. Songs, stories, and celebrations build mutual understanding and respect. All students, not just minority students, can learn from diverse role models.

History: American history and culture teach students about the many individuals who contributed to our country. Discussions of civil rights, immigration, and slavery are significant opportunities for learning about diversity.

Our Stories: Teachers value all students for their unique qualities and talents. In activities like Student of the Week, autobiographies, narratives, and family histories, students come to know and respect one another.

27. How can I divide my class into smaller groups?

It's handy to divide your class into small groups you can call together quickly. Before the year starts, I divide my class into three small groups. I pick balanced groups and run my selections by my students' prior-year teacher.

I call my groups "houses" and name them Hufflepuff, Ravenclaw, and Gryffindor, after houses at Harry Potter's Hogwart's. Large shields of the houses are posted in my classroom.

On the first day, students are assigned to their houses using an old witch hat or sorting hat. There's suspense as names and houses are announced.

Later, I print and laminate small shields that stay on their desktops all year. Students strongly identify with their houses.

Every third day, a given house has special privileges. I post and announce the House of the Day every morning. Among the privileges are:

• Line up and be dismissed first

• Sit in special chairs

• Help teacher as needed

Small groups build communities within a class and help me stay organized.

28. How can I organize and establish centers?

Start small: Begin with one center and gradually add one at a time. Depending on your needs and the size of your room, you might eventually have up to six centers.

Think about purpose: Centers should contain activities students can complete independently. While the class is working at centers, you can call a small group or an individual for instruction.

Grades K–2: Centers provide extra time for math, science, and social studies curricula, since much of the day is devoted to teaching reading. A center might be as simple as a box of Lego® bricks or as complex as a Reader's Theater play or craft project. A listening center with multiple copies of books on CD also works well.

Grades 3–6: Students this age are more independent, so activities can be more open-ended and socially oriented. Science experiments, literature circles, small-group discussions, and logic puzzles adapt well to centers. WebQuests or computer games can be part of center time.

Organize materials: To avoid distractions and interruptions, everything students need should be readily available at a center. It's helpful if a center is organized with bins for papers and supplies.

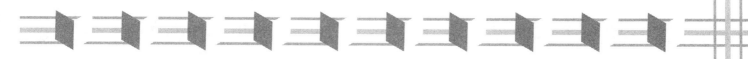

Teach students process: Teach students how to use materials. For younger students, you may teach them how to put a cap on a glue stick. For older students, you may discuss in-depth directions for a project they will do.

Post directions: Display directions in an 8" x 10" clear plastic picture frame with stand. Directions in a frame are visible and easy to change.

Ask an assistant or parent for help: Ask another adult to supervise centers, so activities will proceed more smoothly. This frees you to teach. Parents may be willing to come in once a week.

Evaluate with class: For several weeks, debrief the process daily. Stop centers five minutes early, gather your class together, and ask,

> "What worked well today?"
> "Were there any problems?"
> "How can we work together to make center time better tomorrow?"

29. How can I organize a classroom library?

One benefit of organizing a class library is you'll get to know your book collection. Depending on the size of your library, it may take more than one academic year to organize a class library. I work on my library every summer. Here are several ways I organize books:

Topic: Topic works well if you are organizing nonfiction (e.g., rain forest, magnets, and immigrants).

Genre: Genre is effective for poetry, plays, biographies, and autobiographies.

Series: Second- through sixth-grade students love to read entire series. I display these books on a revolving rack (e.g., A to Z Mysteries, Magic Tree House, and Dear America).

Author: This sorting method works for multiple titles by one author and author studies (e.g., William Steig, Kate DiCamillo, and Kevin Henkes).

Reading level: Level books you will use for small-group reading instruction. If you have a general idea of reading levels for your entire collection, you can steer students toward "just-right books."

30. Do you have ideas for hallway bulletin boards?

Hallway bulletin boards can communicate with an entire school community. Here are some hints for effective displays:

High-quality work from all students: Stress that hallway work is to be of high quality, or "personal best." Make sure all students complete their assignments and have their work posted.

Writing samples: Use bulletin boards as a place to display stories and poems. This is a form of publication. Conference with students to make sure their writing is legible and spelled correctly so it communicates to readers.

Photo displays: If you dissect a shark, put photos of the dissection along with students' drawings of both a shark's inside and outside. When you take a field trip, post photographs of your trip with captions written by students.

Interactive displays: Pose a question or present two sides of an argument and ask passersby their opinions. Put small ballots, pencils, and a ballot box next to your bulletin board. Then tabulate and analyze the data you collect and report back to the community. One interactive bulletin board we did

was about whether or not the Loch Ness Monster exists. Students gathered evidence and wrote persuasive paragraphs both pro and con. This bulletin board stimulated debate.

Three-dimensional displays: In addition to a bulletin board, a 3-D display on a table in front of a bulletin board grabs attention. To go with a bulletin board about Brian Jacques' *Redwall*, we created a cardboard model of Redwall Abbey complete with sculpted clay characters.

Think big: Giant maps and murals attract attention. One sixth-grade teacher transferred a drawing of Martin Luther King, Jr. onto grid paper. His students enlarged it to 8 feet by 8 feet. In another class, second graders painted giant planets and arranged the solar system down a hall.

Teach values: A sixth-grade class made a mural of small fish swimming together and chasing a shark away. This bulletin board sparked conversations among students of all ages about teamwork and bullies.

Invite parents: When a new bulletin board is posted, invite parents to view it. Parents enjoy seeing their children's work and their photos, too.

CHAPTER III

MANAGING A CLASSROOM

Routine Classroom Management

31. How can I manage without an assistant—and still be an effective classroom manager?

While having an assistant can make the varied aspects of managing a classroom easier, you can be an effective classroom manager on your own.

An effective classroom manager is enthusiastic about the subject and students alike. Her positive energy creates interest in her students, who buy into what she is teaching. Her emphasis is on shared tasks, not student behavior. This focus reduces tension and helps students relax so they can learn.

How can you achieve this type of environment? First, have realistic expectations and stick with simple strategies in the beginning. There will be ups and downs as you get to know your students. Teaching is unique because the cast of characters changes annually. Learning about your new students and their parents contributes to the complexity of managing your group. Here are some suggestions to keep in mind:

Demeanor: Stay calm, because your students are looking to you for leadership. If students pick up a nervous, hyper vibe from you, it will make management more challenging.

Tone: Speak with an assertive, measured voice in a low register. Think of your favorite TV news anchor. That's the tone of voice you want to emulate.

Volume: Moderate to low volume makes students quiet down to hear you. As hard as it is, don't raise your voice. Shouting does not promote listening.

Self-control: Show self-control. Don't let frustration or anger creep into your voice. You don't want to let students know they are upsetting you.

The Look: Perfect a beady-eyed scowl at home in front of a mirror. Once students learn your facial expressions, they will understand The Look, which means, "Cut it out, now!"

Teach the rules: It may seem obvious, but make sure students understand your rules and procedures. Students will need repeated, explicit instruction about your expectations. Have a grace period of a few weeks to allow students to learn the rules without consequences for infractions. Consistently follow through with consequences.

Consequences: Consequences are corrections that result from not abiding by rules and procedures.

"You broke something? Then you sweep up the pieces and put them in a trash can."

"You didn't do your homework at home? Then you'll have to do it at school today."

Praise: Use positive reinforcement. Compliment students doing the right things, no matter how small. Praise them by saying, "I like the way you . . ." or "I was glad to see you . . ."

Be specific in the way you praise students. Their classmates will overhear your compliments and learn appropriate behavior.

Positives: Work toward positive behavior. Before I take my class into the hall, I say, "Let's see if we can get a compliment from other teachers today. Let's see if they notice how quiet we are." Chances are another adult will notice positive behavior and praise students.

Ignore: Ignore negative behavior. The less attention you give to negative behavior, the more quickly it will extinguish itself. At times, this is impossible, but ignore what you can.

Paperwork: Honestly, a beginning teacher typically needs to spend three hours per night on paperwork—grading papers, preparing for the following day, completing reports, writing memos, corresponding by e-mail, and so on. Doing this at home allows you to concentrate on teaching students during the school day. However, set a time limit and stick to it. It's important to relax and spend time with family and friends.

Rewards and incentives: Group and individual rewards and incentives are ways to work toward positive behavior. Try group rewards first. There are classes that will work cooperatively for extra recess, pizza parties, or ice cream sundaes. Group rewards are preferable because everyone shares in the reward.

> **TIP:** I found name tag stickers that said "Math Whiz" at an online teacher store. All my students wanted to solve the math problem of the day so they could get a Math Whiz sticker.

Individual incentives are awarded for excellence or improvement in behavior. It may be necessary to have a formal behavior modification plan for a few students. Individual rewards might include stickers, computer time, or free time.

Parents: If a student is involved in one major infraction or several minor situations, contact the student's parents. Tell them what happened and how you are addressing the problem. Ask for their support. A few students need both home and school consequences. Parents may not hold their child accountable, but you are doing your part by keeping them informed.

Consult: There will be students who are so challenging, you will need to consult with a mentor teacher, team leader, or administrator. A guidance counselor, psychologist, or nurse may be a resource for you, too. Do seek help if you need it. Feel confident, knowing you have done your best to address negative behavior.

32. I am replacing a teacher who quit. How can I manage her students?

Over the first weeks, assess the relationship your new students had with their former teacher. They will probably drop little hints. It's not that you should act like someone else, but understanding their relationship will help you know your students.

Find out the rules and procedures that are in place. If you need to supplement class rules with a few of your own, do so within the first week.

It's honest to tell your students things will change. Don't change everything at once, but gradually phase in new routines and activities. Change the room arrangement and add your own special flair to the bulletin boards.

During your first weeks together, you may need to remind your students that you are not their former teacher. They may call you by her name and tell you how much they miss her. Don't take this personally. Acknowledge that it's normal for them to miss their former teacher.

If their teacher is on maternity leave, expect ups and downs over the first six to eight weeks. Keep your expectations of student accomplishments realistic, knowing you will only be their teacher for a few months. After a month or two, invite the teacher to bring her new baby in to meet the class. Make her welcome and let her have center stage. Your acceptance of their former teacher will help you as you continue to build your own relationship with the class.

33. What are the top three things to do for students who finish their work early?

Practice skills: Students can use extra time to practice their spelling words or multiplication facts. Two students can work together quietly on these activities.

Enrichment: Students who regularly finish first enjoy enriching activities. This is not more work. Instead, enrichment might include math puzzles, chess, books, or computer time.

Help others: Every student should have the experience of helping classmates. Those who finish their work early may occasionally be asked to assist a classmate. This is good for both students, as long as the same children are not doing all the assisting.

34. What can I do about students who don't listen?

Try implementing Harry Wong's "Give Me Five," which is explained in detail in *The First Days of School*. Use his suggested steps or make up your own. As students practice, they recite the five steps aloud. Make a poster for your classroom and send a copy of "Give Me Five" home with your students. When you say, "Give me five," your students will respond in the following ways:

- Hands and feet quiet. (Or: Stop and put down what is in my hands.)
- Sit up straight. (Or: Turn toward my teacher.)
- Eyes on the speaker.
- Lips closed.
- Ears listening.

My students move around a lot. Since they aren't always at their desks, I teach them to stop, put down their work, and face me. Students will need to practice the "Give Me Five" steps aloud for several weeks until they memorize the steps. Then you will be able to say, "Give me five," and just count from one to five. The effort you put into teaching the five steps to listening will pay off in the long run. Typically this level of self-control is not required at home so parents may not fully understand. If questions come up, let parents know politely that teaching groups is different than parenting one or two children.

35. Why don't students listen?

There are several reasons students don't listen. Students have trouble listening in the beginning of the year because they don't yet know your voice. It's like imprinting on baby ducklings. They have to learn to respond to your voice and read your facial expressions. You can teach a class to listen by reading aloud to them. As you read expressively, students will learn the meaning of tones and inflections in your voice. They will be learning to listen.

Another reason students don't listen is sometimes parents have not expected them to listen. Stating your rules clearly and often will help students learn what you expect from them.

Here are suggested rules to encourage listening:

- When I'm talking, you are listening.
- Raise a quiet hand to speak. Wait until you are called on to speak.
- When a classmate is speaking, look at that person to show you are listening.
- When you are talking to your classmates, make eye contact to help them listen.

36. What can I do about classroom talkers?

If you have only a few talkers, don't let them hold the entire class hostage. Instead, try these ideas:

Change seating: There are many ways to change seating to stop talkers. Seat talkers close to you so you can redirect them nonverbally. Stand next to their desks. Lightly touch their shoulders or point to what you want them to do. Try a boy-girl pattern to separate talkers. Turn desks so students are facing you, not one another. If you have tables made from groups of desks, separate the desks and arrange them in rows facing the front of the class. You don't want the talkers to have eye contact with one another either. You are not obligated to explain to students why you changed their seats.

Speak privately: Speak with the talkers away from the group. Use a strong voice in a lower register—don't shout—to let them know their behavior is unacceptable and you expect it to change. Spell out the consequences and be sure to follow through consistently. A warning may help students see the urgency of their situation.

Behavior plan: A formal behavior plan with goals like "Raise your hand to speak" may be needed. If you are with the talkers all day, give them chances to earn points in both the morning and afternoon. If students show poor self-control in the morning, they can redeem themselves in the afternoon. Specific rewards are part of a behavior plan.

Time-out: For students in grades K–2 and for older students with severe behavior problems, you may want to designate an area of your classroom for "time out."

Support: Contact the students' parents. Ask your administrator, psychologist, or behavior specialist for support.

37. How can I teach a multi-age combination class?

A multi-age class is like a large family. Since you and students will be together for two or more years, you'll build strong relationships. The increased time together will allow you flexibility. You may feel less pressure to push students because what you don't teach them this year, you'll teach them next year.

Creating a sense of community is especially important in multi-age classrooms. Most students identify with peers of their grade and age, but your students will learn to identify with one another and their class. Place students in groups according to skill level rather than grade or age. Hold class meetings at the beginning and end of each day. Service projects, field trips, routines, and rituals all build community.

The challenging early weeks, during which students adjust to new rules, procedures, and expectations, are minimized. You can't be everywhere at once, so encourage students to help one another. Older students can teach younger students the rules, and you're able to spend more time teaching. Everyone is an expert at something, so accentuate strengths and try not to let a few older students do all the assisting. Students in multi-age classrooms need to be resourceful and independent.

Working with students in two or more grades requires organization. You'll need long-range plans. If students will be with you for three years, create a three-year cycle for science and social studies units. You may teach life science concepts every year, but through studying different animals. You'll also need a three-year cycle of read-aloud books. If you use nonfiction books to teach reading, you'll cover science and social studies concepts during reading class. Accelerate younger math students so they are more in sync with older students. With fewer math groups, you'll have more time with each group. Individualize writing and spelling programs so students can progress at their own speed.

38. What is looping? How can I organize my curriculum so it will work for me?

When a teacher loops with her class, she stays with them for two years. For example, on alternate years she teaches grades two and three.

More than one teacher has to participate in looping for it to work logistically. In the example above, both second- and third-grade teachers agreed to teach both grades.

As with multi-age classrooms, you'll need a comprehensive two-year plan. You will be teaching only one grade per year, but you'll be responsible for covering state standards for grades two and three during the two years you have your students. Consult with grade-level colleagues in both grades to ensure you cover the mandated curriculum.

The advantages of looping are similar to the advantages of teaching a multi-age class. Students and teachers have more time to develop relationships, and the pace can be adjusted to meet individual needs. Another advantage is you'll spend less time teaching rules and procedures in the second year since students already know you and your expectations. Instead, you'll be able to devote more time to teaching. For those students who struggle with transitions to new teachers, looping lets them relax and be ready to learn from the first day.

> **TIP:** In multi-age and looping situations, students will return to the same classroom, so give it a fresh look. Consider rearranging the furniture and changing decor every year so students feel they are in a new classroom.

39. How can I get students to do their homework?

Grades K–2: For primary students, homework is as much form as substance. Young students learn what homework is and develop consistent homework habits. They carry a homework folder back and forth to school and sit down for 10 to 20 minutes per night to complete homework.

Parents find out teachers expect students to practice outside of school. They also discover that supervising homework is one of their parental responsibilities. In addition to monitoring written homework, encourage parents to read aloud nightly as well as listen to their child practice reading.

Most primary students are enthusiastic and motivated to do homework. When they don't complete their homework, it may be that parents aren't providing enough support. You'll need to connect with parents promptly to address homework issues.

Homework can become a battleground. Parents and child may struggle for power over the issue of homework. When that's the case, I advise parents to create a quiet study spot (not at a kitchen table) and set a timer for 20 minutes. Students resist less if there is a routine time and place for homework. When the timer buzzes, parents put homework into the homework folder and write me a brief note. This helps me gauge whether or not an assignment is reasonable and it also prevents power struggles.

For some children, homework time is the only time they spend with their parents during the week, so when you can, make homework light and fun. Occasionally assign activities a parent and child can do together, like taking a nature walk, playing a math game, or doing computer-related research. This will ease the tension between parent and child over homework.

Grades 3–6: I asked a friend who teaches sixth grade how he handles homework, and I'm going to pass on his ideas to you.

First, he stressed the importance of being consistent with follow-through regarding homework policy. Assignments may be modified up-front for special education students, but all students are expected to do their homework. If an exception is made for one individual, soon the whole class will negotiate for exceptions.

Give homework assignments that extend previously taught concepts and lead to new knowledge, rather than assign drill and practice exercises. Assignments that make students think and create are more engaging.

The following day, walk around your classroom and spot-check homework to see that students are at least attempting assignments. If a student tried to do his homework but made mistakes, that's okay. But if a student did not make an attempt, record that in your grade book. As you spot-check homework, students' errors will direct your lesson, and you will address what they don't know.

If a student misses more than two assignments a week, she is assigned to study hall or detention. A student can work her way out of study hall by completing her homework for five consecutive nights. Otherwise she continues to accumulate additional days in study hall.

Once a week (on a different day each week) announce in advance that, the following day, homework will be collected and graded. Grading homework once a week is enough.

When all else fails, ask the student's parents to come in for a conference with their child present. Contacting parents of older students about homework is reserved for students with chronic homework problems. It's advisable to include an administrator in a parent conference if you anticipate difficulty.

Handling Difficult Situations

40. This year I'll be teaching in an open classroom for the first time. Would you give me hints about how to manage in this teaching environment?

A significant difference in an open classroom environment is the proximity to other teachers. This is an advantage if there is collegiality and cooperation among the teachers.

In an open classroom, it's especially important to be honest with colleagues and deal with conflicts and misunderstandings promptly. An assertive, unemotional approach to problem solving will go a long way toward enhancing relationships with coworkers.

Planning: One advantage of an open classroom is you will have colleagues to assist with weekly and long-term planning. As a new team member, you'll work with others on school-wide events, field trips, and parent conference schedules.

Teaching load: Teachers frequently share teaching responsibilities. You may not have to teach as many subjects as you would in a traditional classroom.

Familiarity with students: If you have to be out of class due to a meeting, there will be other teachers who know your students. This is also a plus if you need support with discipline.

Teaching within hearing: You will need to overcome self-conscious feelings about teaching within hearing of other teachers. We all make mistakes and chances are, when you do, another teacher will be aware. Coteachers will overhear your effective lessons, too.

Noise: Depending upon the physical arrangement, an open space can be crowded with students and furniture. Though there may be bookcase dividers or accordion doors, sound travels. Shifting chairs and the low hum of a class at work are magnified. If your class is doing a science experiment while another teacher is giving a spelling test, noise may be a problem. Planning as part of a team may help to minimize scheduling conflicts such as this one.

41. What can I do about bullies?

Find out if your school has an anti-bullying policy. Is there a guidance counselor or psychologist who could meet with the relevant students or with your class as a whole?

I highly recommend reading *The Bully, the Bullied, and the Bystander: From Preschool to High School—How Parents and Teachers Can Help Break the Cycle of Violence* by Barbara Coloroso. Then talk with an administrator about setting up a joint parent-teacher meeting to discuss bullying and explore strategies for curbing this behavior.

Bullying is a complex issue, so you and your colleagues will want to attack it in multiple ways.

> For more questions about bullying here are two sources of information and advice:
> *The Bully, the Bullied, and the Bystander: From Preschool to High School—How Parents and Teachers Can Help Break the Cycle of Violence* by Barbara Coloroso (HarperCollins, 2004)
> *Creating a Bully-Free Classroom* by Carol McMullen (Scholastic, 2005)

Take bullying seriously: Bullies can ruin all kinds of school activities for other students, both in and out of the classroom. More than that, the damage bullies do can affect their targets in deep, long-lasting ways, as we learned after the Columbine tragedy. It's not enough to punish bullies when incidents occur. What's required is a change in the environment and attitudes of all students, particularly bystanders.

Be vigilant: Mobilize the entire school community to stop bullying. All staff members and students need to be alert and prepared to stop a bullying incident.

Increase number of adults: On the playground, increase the ratio of adults to students. A teacher or administrator needs to be present on the playground at all times. Recruit paraprofessionals and parent volunteers to assist those already on duty.

Adults should walk around to monitor behavior and step in promptly to stop conflict. Adults need to make the playground safe for all students. They should not stand at the edge of the playground and chat with one another. When students report incidents, adults need to take them seriously and follow up.

Keep a log: A designated teacher on our playground carries a notebook in which she records the date, adults on duty, and incidents of bullying, exclusion, isolation, and accidents. It helps to have a written record so teachers have accurate data and see patterns of behavior over time. When we meet with parents, it's enlightening for them to see evidence, not just hear anecdotes.

Enlist bystanders: Every morning as part of our class promise my students say, "We stand up for what is right, for ourselves and others." All students need to know they can and should stop bullies. We teach and practice a ready, shouted response, "NO! Stop it right now!" Students are encouraged to stop bullies themselves and seek adult help. We call this "reporting" and stress that students aren't tattling when they tell adults.

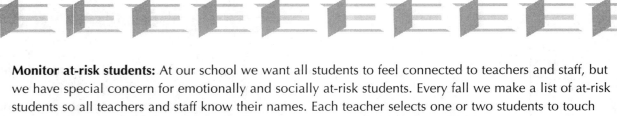

Monitor at-risk students: At our school we want all students to feel connected to teachers and staff, but we have special concern for emotionally and socially at-risk students. Every fall we make a list of at-risk students so all teachers and staff know their names. Each teacher selects one or two students to touch base with in the halls and on the playground. We check in with these students every day and, in recognizing and caring about them, strengthen their connection to us and to the community. Students who feel genuinely cared for are less likely to become bullies or targets.

Use literature: Recently a number of books have been written specifically about bullying, and while they're good, they aren't always the most effective. A book doesn't have to have bully in the title to be about bullying. I find it's more effective if the topic can be incorporated throughout the year as students read and respond to literature. For example, one of my read-aloud chapter books is an animal story, *Poppy* by Avi. Mr. Ocax, a Great Horned Owl, is the villain in *Poppy*. Ocax is a classic bully who embodies attributes of fear, anxiety, and insecurity. As we read, we discuss characteristics of bullies and what makes them target others.

42. My class is the worst-behaved class in the whole school! Now what?

It's a horrible feeling when you think you have the worst class in school. Colleagues can be both judgmental and secretly relieved it's not their class. Their unkind whispering may make you think it's your fault when it's not. Frequently it's just a mix of personalities that creates an unhealthy dynamic with a class, a "perfect storm." Here are two ideas for changing group behavior:

Grades K–2: One strategy for changing group behavior is a marble jar. Get a mason jar and a bag of marbles. Tell students two or three behaviors you will look for, like staying seated or whispering quietly. When you see a student exhibiting that behavior add a marble to the jar. Praise the student and encourage others to behave appropriately and add marbles to the jar. It's important that the marble jar be on a shelf where the whole class can see it. When the jar is full of marbles, the entire class gets a treat like ice cream cups or one hour of choice time. The reward has to be one that is enticing for the class.

From experience I know this works. Students start to remind one another about their behavior. There is much interest in the marbles as they accumulate in the jar: "Look, now the jar is more than half full!"

Grades 3–6: Another way to work with a difficult class is to set up a behavior plan for all your students. First select two specific goals, such as staying seated during writing time or raising one's hand to speak.

Then create a small chart that lists the goals down the side and the days of the week across the top. Shrink the chart to 3" x 5", make laminated copies, and tape them to the desktops. Establish the number of points required to meet a weekly goal. Select a group reward, like 30 minutes of extra recess. During the week, add small stickers when you see students meeting goals. On Friday afternoon, everyone who has enough points earns the reward. Those who don't make it stay in their classroom and complete a cause-and-effect graphic organizer explaining why they did not achieve their goal and what they plan to do differently the following week. Using a graphic organizer such as this helps students focus and address their shortcomings. If necessary, especially for younger students, you may want to try a T-chart labeled "Last Week" and "Next Week."

I have used this strategy successfully. In the beginning, a few students reach the goal, but gradually others join them, especially when the reward is desirable. It takes several months for this to work. I kept track of who met the goal each week to make sure everyone participated in the reward.

43. How can I stop yelling?

Many teachers raise their voices occasionally, but as you have discovered, yelling is counterproductive. Since you already have established a pattern of yelling, you will need to break your pattern.

Grades K–2: You might calmly say to younger students:

> "I've been raising my voice, but beginning today I'm not going to raise my voice or talk over your talking. In fact, I'm going to lower my voice and speak softly so you'll have to listen carefully. If you talk while I'm talking, then you are taking my time. If you take my class time then I will take your recess."

Announcing to your class your intention to speak softly means your students will hold you accountable. Spelling out consequences for continued talking holds students accountable.

Grades 3–6: With older students, don't say anything to the students; just stop yelling. After three days, ask students if they notice anything different. This will lead to a group discussion. Mention to friends and family that you are trying not to yell and ask them to check in with you periodically and hold you accountable.

If you don't yell, how will you get their attention? You need to cultivate a commanding presence. This is not yelling. It is letting students know you are in charge. You assert leadership with body language. Stand up straight and move calmly and confidently around the room. Be well organized and change quickly from subject to subject. Consider increasing your pace. Avoid downtime by having plenty for students to do. The better you organize and plan, the more confidence your students will have in your leadership.

If you stand or sit on a high stool, you will have better control than if you sit behind a desk. If you circulate around your classroom, you will be closer to your students, and it will feel natural to speak in a normal tone of voice.

44. How can I reach unmotivated students?

At its core, teaching is about building relationships. Before you can teach a resistant, unmotivated student, you'll need to first build your relationship with her. Right now this may be the last thing you want to do. You know her as an unmotivated student, but as you strengthen your relationship, you'll understand her in a new light.

Get to know the student as a person, her personality, likes, and dislikes. Based on her interests, check out a library book you think she'll like and leave it on her desk. Ask her one or two personal questions each day during an independent work period. Call on her at least three times a day. Even if she refuses to respond, you'll show her you hope she'll join the discussion.

Find out about the student's home life. Information about her family will give you valuable insight into this student. If possible speak to the parents or invite them to school to meet you.

Spend non-academic time with this student. Play cards, chat, and observe on the playground. Occasionally eat lunch with her.

Students need to feel relaxed and comfortable to learn. You can create a calm, caring atmosphere in which this student will thrive.

45. What can I do about a student who is defiant and unresponsive?

Grades K–2: A young student who is unable to talk about his feelings when he is angry or sad may stop talking. This willful, sulking behavior can be frustrating. Sometimes students don't talk because they don't have a repertoire of feeling words. Teaching feeling words to an entire class and role-playing how facial expressions show feelings helps students develop their vocabularies. A poster with photos of children with a variety of facial expressions allows this student to simply point to how he's feeling. Or you can identify his feelings for him: "I see you're feeling angry. Let's talk about what happened."

Students in grades K–2 need a warm, nurturing teacher to help them open up. A structured, predictable classroom will encourage these students to trust their teacher and relax.

Grades 3–6: Tell an upset, angry, or unresponsive student you'd like to talk about what happened when he is calm: "I can tell you're upset right now. I'm going to help other students. When you are feeling calm and in control, we'll talk about what upset you."

> For strategies that work both at home and school, read *The Explosive Child* by Ross W. Greene (HarperCollins, 2005).

Then let him visit the restroom or just sit for a few minutes. After about 10 to 15 minutes, check back with the student. Engage him in casual conversation and then hear him out. Help the student solve his problem, if possible. Make a plan together to avoid this behavior the next time he is upset. Agree on a signal he can give you if he is feeling overwhelmed. Let him know it is all right to leave the classroom for a few minutes to cool down. He could run an errand for you or take a short break in the library.

If this behavior happens on a daily basis, consult your school psychologist.

46. I only have nine students. Why am I having so many discipline problems?

A class of nine students is too small. There are so few viewpoints expressed in a small class that it's difficult to have interesting discussions. There may not be the cultural or ethnic diversity a larger group would have. There are fewer friendship possibilities, so students may form cliques or exclusive twosomes, both of which negatively impact a class community.

Sometimes one or two dominant students with behavior problems can take over the class. There are not enough students to serve as a counterweight. That may account for the discipline problems in your class.

You need to deal with the dominant students' behavior first. Try talking with them individually. If your principal is supportive, you can meet with them in her office. This will impress students with the seriousness of their actions. Call their parents and arrange for parent-teacher conferences. Maybe your principal will sit in on the conferences.

> Steps to Respect (for primary grades) and Second Step (for intermediate grades) are social skills programs from Committee for Children (http://www.cfchildren.org). Among skills taught are anger management, self-control, and empathy.

Your entire class would benefit from a social skills program (see information at right) to help them learn how to form a cohesive community. Social skills training twice a week plus community meetings at the beginning and end of every day will help your class develop in positive ways.

47. I got off on the wrong foot. Can I retrain students in November?

The time to establish rules and routines is the first six to eight weeks of school. When students show by their behavior that they understand the rules and accept your authority as their leader, there can be a gradual release of responsibility on your part.

Having rules is a positive step, but as you've discovered, it's consistent follow-through that makes your classroom run smoothly. You may not need any additional rules if you enforce the rules you already have.

Since your management of the group has broken down, you need to have a heart-to-heart chat with your class. Have this talk in the morning. Morning Meeting would be an appropriate time to discuss their behavior. Let your class know that their behavior is unacceptable and must change.

It will be a challenge to convince your students that you are going to be consistent. The younger your students, the easier it will be for them to make a shift in late fall. Your students will test you, and you will have to follow through 100% of the time. This is tough to do, especially when you are not used to it. Students love to negotiate. They are apt to think rules don't apply to them or their unique situation. You must apply your rules fairly to everyone, with no exceptions.

48. How can I manage an autistic student?

Autism is a spectrum disorder. Because there is a broad range of symptoms, there's no one way to manage an autistic student. Autistic individuals I have known have each had unique symptoms, from Asperger's Syndrome quirkiness to out-of-bounds behavior (screaming, removing clothes, running from school property), to developmental delays.

Due to autism's complexity, managing an autistic student is not something a classroom teacher should do on her own. It takes a team of specialists to create a program for an autistic student. Parents are valued team members since they know their child better than anyone. Team members may include a psychologist, occupational therapist, physical therapist, speech and language pathologist, nurse, special educator, classroom teacher, individual assistant/aide, parents, and principal. Sometimes an autism specialist is called in to consult with a special education team.

> For information from experts, visit the following Web sites:
>
> American Academy of Pediatrics:
> http://www.aap.org
>
> National Autism Association:
> http://www.nationalautismassociation.org
>
> U.S. Autism and Asperger Association:
> http://www.usautism.org

Chances are your autistic student already has an Individual Education Plan (IEP) and works with several specialists. Read her IEP and consult with her parents and your special education team. Ask them for strategies and materials to help you work with this student. If your student is not on an IEP, refer her to your special education department for an evaluation.

While special education students are placed in a "least restrictive environment," there are autistic students who need a substantially separate program. If your entire class is suffering due to one student's behavior, bring this to the attention of an administrator.

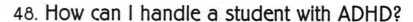

48. How can I handle a student with ADHD?

You will need a large bag of tricks to work productively with an ADHD student. While many strategies work for ADHD students, no strategy is effective for long because this student loses interest quickly. Once the novelty has worn off, you will need to adopt a new strategy.

All students in grades K–2 need frequent breaks and chances to move. Typical students in grades 3–6 are able to sit at a desk all day. Students with ADHD will need special support and accommodations, but what's good for an ADHD student will benefit his more typical classmates as well.

A highly structured and predictable classroom works well for all students, but especially students with ADHD. Post and preview the day's schedule with your class. If there are changes in routine due to an assembly or visitor, make sure everyone knows in advance. An ADHD student feels out of control, but a structured, predictable setting offers him a measure of control.

To help all students pay attention, keep your room decor simple. It's easy for a classroom to become cluttered, so reevaluate periodically. Put away items you are not using, get rid of extra furniture, and cover open shelves with curtains.

Behavior charts are not effective with ADHD students. The delay in gratification a behavior chart requires is too difficult for them. Instant rewards, like stickers, work better. Here are other suggestions to try with ADHD students:

Seating: Seat this student near you in the front of the room, away from distractions. If necessary, use cardboard dividers to make a study carrel.

Desk: Help an ADHD student clean his desk and organize his materials once or twice a week.

Materials: Give assistance and extra time for an ADHD student to get out necessary books and materials for a lesson. Ask a classmate to help him find the correct page.

> For more tips and strategies for teachers and parents, read *A Mind at a Time* by pediatrician Dr. Mel Levine (Simon & Schuster, 2002). You may also want to visit his Web site, All Kinds of Minds: http://www.allkindsofminds.org
>
> Since ADHD runs in families, parents may be affected. Consider suggesting these resources:
>
> *Driven to Distraction: Recognizing and Coping With Attention Deficit Disorder From Childhood Through Adulthood* by Edward M. Hallowell and John J. Ratey (Simon & Schuster, 1995)
>
> CHADD (Children and Adults With Attention Deficit/Hyperactivity Disorder: http://www.chadd.org

To-do list: Type and laminate a to-do list for the top of the student's desk. This will remind her what you expect of her.

Time: This student will need more time than her classmates to collect her thoughts and respond to a question, so increase your wait-time when you call on her. Don't let classmates answer for her. This student also needs more time to complete her written work and help getting started on written tasks. A timer or stopwatch may help.

Nonverbal redirection: It's tempting to constantly verbally redirect this student, because he needs it. If you can work out nonverbal signals, you won't have to single him out as often.

Sensory breaks: Make this student your messenger and send him on errands. Allow extra bathroom trips. Check with an occupational therapist or P.E. teacher who may be able to offer an ADHD student breaks during the day.

Fiddle toys and gadgets: It seems counterintuitive, but fiddle toys sometimes help students focus. Have a box of fiddle toys like small Nerf balls and plastic toys. Allow an ADHD student to select a different fiddle toy every morning. A large elastic band stretched between the front legs of his chair, a wiggle cushion for his chair seat, and a slant board for writing also help. Ask your occupational therapist about these and other gadgets.

Medication: I mention medication last because some parents are reluctant to consider it. There are now several medications, and not all are stimulants, but I can understand parents' reticence. Negative press about ADHD medications concerns parents. Side effects also worry them.

At my school, teachers don't mention medication to parents of ADHD students. The most I say if a parent brings up medication is, "You might discuss this with your pediatrician." In my experience, medicine sometimes works miraculously. When medicine works, an ADHD student will change within a day. But medicine is not for everyone, and there are other ways to cope with ADHD.

50. What can I do about a student who lies?

Lying should be taken seriously, often more seriously than the infraction that led to dishonesty. For example, if a student draws on a bathroom wall and then lies about it, the lie is at least as important as the scribbling. It is important to handle lying differently depending on the student's age.

Grades K–1: Helping young students learn the difference between what's real and what's not is part of teaching about honesty. Students under age 6 have difficulty distinguishing between fantasy and reality and like to exaggerate. What may sound like a lie to you may just be fantasy. Students at this age also may lie to avoid punishment or earn adult approval.

Grades 2–6: An older student may be afraid of making mistakes or disappointing you. He may be interested in impressing you or his classmates. Set limits and let students know you won't tolerate lies.

> Here's a good source of information about child development and behavior problems:
> American Academy of Pediatrics:
> http://www.aap.org

As with all discipline, logical consequences for lying need to be clearly spelled out from the beginning. You will need to follow through consistently with consequences.

If a student has a pattern of lying, inform his parents and your school psychologist or guidance counselor. You may request a parent-teacher conference so parents understand the seriousness of this issue. Chronic liars may have serious emotional problems.

Honesty is an appropriate topic for social skills lessons for the whole class, and that way one student isn't singled out. Of course it's important for you to set an example of honesty, too.

51. When I have a substitute, my students' behavior gets worse. What can I do?

Your responsibility as a classroom teacher is to provide the best possible learning environment for your students every day. This includes what happens when you are absent. However, we all know most students don't behave as well for a substitute as they do for their classroom teacher.

When you know in advance you will be absent for a meeting or personal day, tell your students the day before your absence and ask for their cooperation. Remind your students you are expecting them to be on their best behavior.

Some principals ask classroom teachers to make up generic packets or file folders with information and teaching materials for a substitute. Put this folder near your plan book.

Leave a note to your class on the blackboard promising them a treat if you get a good report from their substitute teacher. Or write a note, make copies, and place notes on their desks the evening before your absence. Keep the treat a surprise.

If you have a choice, select a substitute teacher you know is a good classroom manager. Explain to your substitute in writing that you expect her to leave a note about your students' behavior and to check off all lessons she completes. Prepare detailed plans. Leave extra packets of activities and extra read-aloud books. You want to keep students busy.

Ask a colleague or administrator to look in on your class in your absence. Tell them you want honest feedback about your students' behavior. Prepare for bad news, just in case. Ask your colleagues for their suggestions.

In case of a sudden illness, accident, or other emergency, be sure to call your school. Follow accepted protocol for getting a replacement. E-mail your lesson plans to a colleague or your principal.

When you return to school, debrief the previous day with your class. Ask students how they liked their substitute, what they learned, how they behaved, and what, if anything, they would do differently in the future.

52. I'm overwhelmed trying to "get it all in." What should I do?

Many teachers feel overwhelmed at times. There are a number of factors outside your control that could contribute to this situation. For example, this may be due to students' immaturity and lack of readiness or perhaps due to learning issues among your students. Group dynamics plays a role in pacing. Or maybe you've slowed down for a new assistant whom you're training while you teach. Whatever the reasons, you feel you're falling behind.

Consider the time you have left and revise your yearly plan. Remember that reading, writing, and math are key subjects. If you can't teach it all, establish priorities. You may have to shorten units or spend more time teaching certain subjects in order to cover the material. From now on, check your progress at the end of each unit to see if you need to further revise your goals.

Look at the amount of downtime your students have and consider ways to increase efficiency. Make sure students have an assignment to do as soon as they enter your classroom. Move quickly and purposefully from one activity to another. Limit free time. You may be able to recapture a few minutes of lost time each day.

You'll cover more material by making simple changes in your curriculum. Use nonfiction books for read-alouds and reading-group instruction, and you'll teach science and social studies while you teach reading. Set up a listening center, games, and independent activities that are content-based and correlate with your units. Arrange field trips and guest speaker visits to liven up your curriculum. Ask parent volunteers to assist during independent work time so you can meet with individuals or small groups.

Mention your pacing problem to your colleagues, because together you may decide to break up this group next year.

53. I'm a new teacher and I've had a rough year. I'd like to end the year on a positive note. Do you have any ideas for me?

Teachers have so many wonderful plans at the beginning of the school year. All the pencils are sharp, and none of the crayons are broken. Parents are sure we'll work miracles, and students are full of excitement. But by March or April, we know there isn't time to do all we hoped to accomplish. We're tired, and so are our students and their parents. That's when disappointment can set in.

March and April are months with regrets and misgivings for many teachers, both new and veteran. To one degree or another, we feel we have failed our students. I feel this every spring.

Here are a few ideas to help counteract these feelings:

Positive self-talk: So I won't be in a funk for the rest of the year, I repeat to myself any little successes I may have had during past months.

Enhance communication: One way to overcome negative feelings is to enhance communication with parents. Tell them in your weekly newsletter about the positive things their children have been doing. If you don't have a newsletter, start one.

List memories: With your students' help, make a list of all memorable events, entitled "We will remember . . ." Make copies and send them home. Parents will realize the effort you put into your teaching, and you'll end the year on a positive note.

Plan for next year: Planning for the next school year helps, too. Look through catalogs and highlight items you want to purchase. Consider alternate ways to organize your reading groups or desks.

> ### EXAMPLES OF POSITIVE SELF-TALK
> - I'm doing my best.
> - I bring my own uniqueness to my work.
> - I'm special.
> - I'm still growing and developing as a teacher.
> - I'm more than just a job description.
> - There are parents and students who appreciate my efforts.
> - We all make mistakes. I can learn from my mistakes.
> - Next school year will be easier.
> - Next year I'll do things differently.

Meet incoming students: Get acquainted with students who will be entering your grade. Once you have a list of your incoming class, invite the students to visit your classroom and give them a summer reading list to keep them reading. They're looking forward to moving up and having you as their teacher.

54. I'm having doubts about my ability to control my class. Should I leave teaching?

I know that out-of-control feeling. Hang in there; don't give up yet.

You need to take your power back. It's not too late, but address your power imbalance right away. The longer students have the upper hand, the tougher it will be for you to regain control. To get your power back, you're going to need to come up with a new discipline system. Have a talk with your class to explain your new system. Then implement it even-handedly and consistently. If you are consistent, it may take three or four weeks for your new system to work.

Your students must come to see you as their leader. To establish your leadership you will need a combination of positive rewards and negative consequences. If you have tried rewards, and they did

not work, stop them for now and develop a progression of negative consequences. Discuss your list of consequences with an administrator before introducing them to your class.

If there are one or two ringleaders, take them aside and speak with them individually. Make sure they understand they will be held accountable. You may also want to speak with their parents by phone or in person.

Enforcing rules is more than half the battle, as you know. You cannot make exceptions, back down, or cut students slack. They have to learn you mean what you say. When you correct students, do so calmly in a matter-of-fact tone of voice. Do not plead or apologize.

Planning may be part of your problem. It takes years to plan effective units of study, so don't be too hard on yourself. It's not uncommon for new teachers to plan night by night. Do keep working away at it, and remind yourself that next year will be better. Keep a notebook of your successes so you can retain the best of what you have taught for next year.

Collaboration, working along with students as you explore and learn, is a worthy goal. Before collaboration can begin, there must be mutual respect and a calm, controlled environment. Once you become the acknowledged leader, you will be able to collaborate with your students and gradually release responsibility to them.

A SPECIAL NOTE ABOUT TAKING CARE OF YOURSELF

Try these simple strategies to take care of yourself. They will not only benefit you personally, but they will also help you be a better teacher.

Get enough rest: A good night's sleep will make your day brighter!

Eat well-balanced meals and drink plenty of water: Now is not the time for a crash diet.

Exercise: Mild exercise like walking or more vigorous exercise like tennis will help you cope with stress.

Find a listener: A close friend or family member who is outside education but knows you well may listen to you "vent." A counselor may also be a resource for you.

Work in some quiet time: Yes, you have to work hard and bring work home, but give yourself an hour each day to relax. If you have young children, this may mean having a quiet time early in the morning.

CHAPTER IV

ASSESSING STUDENT PROGRESS

55. What's the difference between a formative and summative assessment?

A formative assessment measures learning that is in progress. A summative assessment measures academic gains.

A formative assessment shapes and informs your teaching. Reading inventories, writing activities, quizzes, and class discussions can be formative assessments. You uncover what students are learning and adjust your teaching to meet their unique needs. Formative assessments are primarily for you, although you may report results to students and parents. You may decide to use other teaching strategies and/or materials as you clarify misconceptions and reteach students.

Summative assessments are traditional tests. A summative assessment is a summary of what students have learned. Examples of summative assessments are standardized tests and unit tests.

56. How should I set up my grading system?

Before establishing a grading system, know your school's homework and grading policies and become familiar with the report card format. You'll also need to know your principal and team leader's preferences with regard to sharing information with parents on report cards and in parent-teacher conferences.

Grades K–2: Grading systems for K–2 students are descriptive and give an overall picture of students. Students are tested at intervals throughout the school year to assess their academic progress in reading and math. Test results are meant to inform instruction but aren't always shared with parents. An emphasis on reading and math assessments means learning differences and disabilities can be diagnosed and remedied while students are young. Some schools have homework for K–2 students. Report cards typically have checklists or rubrics rather than letter grades.

Grades 3–6: Regular assessments in all subject areas focus on specific accomplishments and hold students accountable for their academic progress. Students take statewide reading tests annually to ensure they progress toward reading proficiency. Test results are usually shared with parents. Many schools have nightly homework for students in grades 3–6. Report cards are likely to have letter grades or percentages. Conferences may include students as well as parents.

57. Can you advise me on grade-book software and online grading programs?

First, check with an administrator to see if there is already a grading program in use school-wide. Next, ask colleagues what grading program they use because it is easier if you all use the same program. If no one is using a grading program but you want one, do an online search. I found several online grading programs, some of which are free and others are by subscription. Check office supply and computer stores for grading software.

58. How can I help my students become good test takers?

Good teaching every day makes students good test takers. Setting high expectations, demanding quality work, and enforcing rules consistently all contribute to positive test results. A calm, well-organized classroom in which you and your students are fully engaged in learning leads to success on tests. Students who value practice and hard work take tests in stride.

Grades K–2: Students this age take few, if any, standardized tests, but they learn what it means to take a test. As you introduce students to spelling tests and short quizzes, they learn to listen and follow directions. They also learn that test taking has its own protocol. Here are test conditions with which young students will become familiar:

- Uncluttered, quiet room with lots of natural light
- Sharp pencils, erasers, grips, highlighters, numberlines, etc.
- Desks or tables separated from one another and facing forward
- Desktop dividers or study carrels
- Clean desktops
- Book for those who finish the test early

Grades 3–6: By third grade, students understand a test environment. Sample questions from previous tests, usually available online, familiarize students with the test format.

Students in grades 3–6 are ready to learn specific test-taking techniques like:

- Answer all questions. Don't leave any responses blank.
- Use process of elimination to narrow choices.
- Respond using complete sentences.
- Reread the passage to answer comprehension questions.
- Watch the time. Don't spend too much time on any one question.
- Use a highlighter, if one is permitted.
- Show your work when solving math problems. Label your answers.
- Proofread your work. Ask yourself, "Does this answer make sense?"

Special education students: If you have students on individual education plans, be sure they receive the accommodations specified in their IEPs. They may be entitled to the following:

- Separate room
- Extended time
- One-to-one assistance
- Repeated and clarified instructions
- Calculator, ruler, etc.
- Frequent breaks
- Test broken into smaller chunks

59. How can I help my students feel comfortable before and during the state tests?

Try to appear calm and relaxed. Students look to you as their leader and will copy your behavior and attitude. Create a quiet, peaceful atmosphere for testing by separating desks and turning them so students are facing you. Use cardboard dividers to shield students who are easily distracted. Make sure students have the necessary materials on their desks (pencil, eraser, grip, etc.)—and books in case they finish early.

The following ideas may sound simple but they really work.

Lights: The human brain prefers natural light, so open shades and turn off half the fluorescent lights.

Bathroom: Make sure everyone visits the bathroom ahead of time.

Snack: About 20 minutes before the test, offer students a snack like orange juice and pretzels. A mix of salty and sweet foods wakes up their brains. Snacks are important, as some children don't eat breakfast.

Exercise: Right before students sit down for their test, lead them in exercises, like jumping jacks, stretching exercises, or Brain Gym.

Water: Make sure students have water bottles by their desks.

Cheer: Recite a cheer before the test begins. "Two, four, six, eight! On the test, we'll do great!"

Visualization: Ask students to sit down and close their eyes. Guide your class through a visualization in which students see themselves completing the test successfully. This will calm students and help them get ready for the test.

Pause: One teacher I know has students put down their pencils five minutes after they start the test. She tells her students, "Now that you've started this test, breathe deeply and relax for a second. You're going to do well on the test."

60. How can I analyze the results of our scores on the statewide tests?

As you read this year's test results, look at last year's test results for this cohort of students. This will place their scores in the context of their past performance. To keep test results in perspective, look at the previous year's test results for your grade. Also compare your class's performance to that of other classes in your district and state.

If an item analysis is provided along with your test results, examine it carefully. If you don't have an item analysis, you can analyze data yourself by looking for patterns in incorrect answers and areas of strength and weakness in your students' performance. An item analysis is a check on your teaching; it reveals concepts and skills you need to emphasize in the future. For example, you may find you need to spend additional time teaching students to write in complete sentences or answer higher-level thinking questions. Pay special attention to the data for those who have low scores.

There can be many reasons for poor scores, so consider underlying causes for students who struggled with the test. Struggling readers may have difficulty reading math problems. Students who don't know multiplication facts may make careless errors and take too much time on certain questions. Students who have difficulty with written expression may have trouble explaining their mathematical thinking. There are also emotional, social, and family issues that affect a student's performance.

One reason students have difficulty is due to poor questions. There may be occasional problems with wording, directions, or format. Not all errors are a student's fault. Bring poor test questions to the attention of an administrator.

Before you share test results with parents, be sure you understand results for each student. All

students have areas of relative strength, and you'll need to be able to articulate each individual's strengths. Check with your administrator and colleagues about how and when to share test results with parents. Some schools may invite parents to come in to discuss test results while others may send results home in the mail.

Take time to reflect on your teaching. Ask yourself what you can do differently next time to prepare your students better. Don't beat yourself up, but do resolve to address weak areas in your teaching.

61. Can you advise me about midyear and end-of-year assessments?

When students are achieving on or above grade level, you can measure reading and math skills at the beginning, middle, and end of the year. A back-to-school assessment uncovers knowledge gained and retained over the summer. You'll use these results to place students in small, skills-based math and reading groups. A midyear test monitors progress to ensure students make academic gains. An end-of-year assessment sets the stage for next year's teachers to plan for your students.

You may want to test students right before report cards and parent conferences so you'll have up-to-date information when reporting to parents. You may also be asked to give unit and chapter tests.

Monitor special education students and others who struggle academically on a weekly to monthly basis. Special education students may grow in small increments, so look for subtle signs of forward movement. Praising their progress may motivate these students to continue studying.

As to which tests to give, consult your reading specialist, curriculum coordinator, and grade-level colleagues. Usually, certain specific tests are administered across the grades in a school, and it's important for continuity that all teachers give the same tests.

62. What advice can you give me about report card comments?

Be positive: The most important element in a report card comment is tone. Establish an accepting, kind tone by stating things in a positive manner. If you are tempted to say something negative, turn the thought around and give it a positive spin.

Make an outline: Consider how you will structure what you want to say and make a list or brief outline. Prioritize your list from most to least important.

Use data: Use assessment results and quotes from writing samples to support your conclusions. Using data gives objectivity to your comments.

Tell the truth: Parents need to know the truth about their child's academic progress. It's possible to tell the truth in a positive way.

Be diplomatic: You want to be honest, but remain diplomatic. Put yourself in the parents' place as you re-read your comments. Rewrite the comments if they sound too pointed or argumentative.

Avoid anecdotes: Anecdotes, even funny ones, are more suitable for conversation. It's difficult to write anecdotes well and they can sound inappropriate in a report card comment. Remember your comments may become part of a student's permanent record and follow him or her for years to come.

Revise and edit: There's nothing worse than reading report card comments that are full of misspellings and grammatical errors. As educators we need to check and recheck our writing for clarity and accuracy. When in doubt, ask a colleague to check your work, before you submit your comments to an administrator. In many schools an administrator reads all report card comments, so you may be asked to make further revisions.

CHAPTER V

PLANNING CURRICULUM

Reading

63. What is a balanced literacy program?

The National Reading Panel (http://www.nationalreadingpanel.org) has identified five elements of reading: phonics, phonemic awareness, fluency, comprehension, and vocabulary. A balanced literacy program addresses these five elements and encompasses reading, writing, spelling, and speaking. This approach requires at least two hours per day during which there are reading and writing workshops, guided reading instruction, direct instruction in phonics and phonemic awareness, read-alouds, and independent reading.

> For more information about guided reading, grades K–2 teachers can read *Guided Reading: Good First Teaching for All Children* by Irene C. Fountas and Gay Su Pinnell (Heinemann, 1996). Grades 3–6 teachers can read *Guiding Readers and Writers: Teaching Comprehension, Genre, and Content Literacy* by Irene C. Fountas and Gay Su Pinnell (Heinemann, 2001).

64. When should I begin meeting with reading groups?

Grades K–2: In primary grades, students are learning school format, behavior, and rules. In the beginning of the year, it's wise to take several weeks to teach rules and procedures before beginning reading groups. During the first weeks of school, read aloud and discuss books several times a day. Keeping the entire class together will give you a sense of the group and give the group a chance to form into a community. Assess students individually for skills in phonics, phonemic awareness, fluency, and comprehension. Sometime between the third and fifth week, you'll be ready to begin reading groups.

Grades 3–6: In middle and upper elementary grades, begin reading groups as soon as you can. Aim for the second week of school. Students are old enough to have absorbed school rules and are capable of quickly learning class routines and procedures. It's important to begin teaching immediately to capitalize on older students' initial enthusiasm. Some students progress significantly in the fall, so begin teaching as soon as possible.

65. How can I find uninterrupted time to meet with reading groups?

It's tricky to find uninterrupted time to meet with reading groups. Set aside an hour a day and plan to meet with three reading groups. Three reading groups are enough for any teacher to plan and organize. Meet with each group for 15 to 20 minutes.

While you're meeting with reading groups, you'll need to have planned activities for the rest of the class. Ideally, these activities will be quiet and independent. If you have an assistant or parent volunteer, she can supervise the class while you meet with small groups. If you don't have an assistant, teach your students not to interrupt you during a reading group meeting. Ask students to write their questions and problems on sticky notes and answer them in between reading group meetings.

66. How can I organize my Readers' Workshop?

A literacy block typically lasts two to two and a half hours per day. The reading part of literacy lasts about one to one and a half hours.

Activities you might do with an entire class include an interactive read aloud, word work/word building, or a spelling or phonics mini-lesson.

Small-group activities include small-group reading instruction, listening centers and reading games, spelling practice and using computer software or online activities

The presence of other adults will help Readers' Workshop go more smoothly. If you have an assistant, he can supervise while you work with small groups for reading instruction, or you can recruit parent volunteers to work during Readers' Workshop once a week. If you're fortunate to have three adults, set up a workstation for additional small-group instruction.

67. How can I set up a Reading Buddies program?

All you need are two teachers who are willing and have time for their classes to meet. Arrange with a colleague who teaches younger (or older) students to partner in a Reading Buddies program. I asked a kindergarten teacher if he'd like my second graders as reading buddies. My students were paired with his kindergarteners and read to them for ten minutes each week. Before our visits, students practiced with one another, and I coached them on read-aloud techniques. They were proud of their reading and developed friendships with their reading buddies.

68. What can I do about a struggling first-grade reader?

The emphasis on getting students to read early and fluently means teachers feel pressure and responsibility when first graders don't read as well as they think first graders should.

Most students read when they are developmentally ready. Students learn at different rates and in different ways. With support, a student who struggles in first grade may overcome his difficulties.

There are influences in a child's life outside of school that contribute to his reading readiness. Parents who spend time in conversation with their child and read to him are a powerful, positive influence. Enlist the struggling reader's parents in helping him learn to read.

Primary-grade teachers can identify students who will struggle with reading. While there is no need to panic, if you do suspect reading disabilities or emotional problems are obstacles to reading, seek advice from a reading specialist, psychologist, or special educator. Otherwise, an eclectic approach in a literature-rich classroom may be enough to make this student a reader. Many teachers and parents agree there's an element of magic in learning to read.

A strong reading program includes:

- Small (10 to 15 minutes) doses of phonics every day. I use Lexia, a computer program, and Great Leaps, a one-to-one program administered by an assistant

- Small-group reading instruction in groups based on reading fluency

> For extra support, look into these resources:
>
> As part of a guided reading program:
>
> *Phonics Lessons: Letters, Words, and How They Work* by Gay Su Pinnell and Irene C. Fountas (Heinemann, 2003)
>
> *Word Matters: Teaching Phonics and Spelling in the Reading/Writing Classroom* by Gay Su Pinnell and Irene C. Fountas (Heinemann, 1998)
>
> For a handwriting program:
>
> *Handwriting Without Tears* by Jan Z. Olsen (http://www.hwtears.com)

- Daily work in building words and spelling principles

- Handwriting instruction, daily at first, and later several times a week (Although writing usually develops after reading, there is a symbiotic relationship between reading and writing.)

- Fluency practice like Reader's Theater, choral reading, and singing

- Ten minutes a day of independent, silent reading or "whisper reading"

- Interactive read-alouds twice daily with both picture and chapter books

- Supportive special educator who provides supplemental reading instruction and assesses student progress monthly

- Parents who read to their child nightly and listen to her read

- A positive teacher who loves literature and reading

69. What can I do about older students who read on a first-grade level?

Hi–Lo books: Look for high-interest, low-vocabulary books, or hi-lo books. They're written on a low reading level about subjects that interest older readers.

Nonfiction: Carefully chosen, nonfiction books written for first and second graders may work. Photos in nonfiction books make simple texts appropriate for older students.

> Scholastic publishes several resources featuring hi-lo reading passages, including:
>
> *Hi-Lo Passages to Build Comprehension* (for Grades 3-4 and Grades 5-6) by Michael Priestley
>
> *Hi-Lo Nonfiction Passages for Struggling Readers* (for Grades 4-5 and Grades 6-8) by Scholastic.

Interest inventory: Create an interest inventory and find out what excites your students. Weight-lifting? Monster trucks? Snowboarding? Once you know their interests, search for books to which they'll connect.

Newspapers and magazines: Use articles from magazines and newspapers about subjects of interest. If necessary, rewrite articles in simple language. Photos that accompany articles provide needed picture support for beginning readers.

Students' stories: Students might write their own stories to accompany magazine or newspaper photos. Most readers can read what they write. Writing practice, even at a sentence level will enhance literacy skills. Students might share PowerPoint presentations of their stories.

Web sites: Web sites like www.readinga-z.com have nonfiction books on a wide range of reading levels. You'll find books to download, lesson plans, worksheets, assessments, and benchmark books on this subscription site. Web sites about topics of interest may have abridged articles your students will enjoy reading.

70. How can I select appropriate books for advanced young readers?

Young readers and their parents tend to emphasize the length and complexity of books. A parent may say, "My son was reading Harry Potter at age 5."

It's important to select books carefully, taking into consideration a student's social and emotional development as well as his reading level. Although a kindergarten student may be able to read Harry Potter, that doesn't mean it's appropriate for him. Young readers may not have enough life experience to comprehend every book they can read.

Here are appropriate chapter books for younger readers.

Animal stories: Young readers understand and enjoy books with animals as main characters like *Stuart Little* by E.B. White and *Poppy and Rye* by Avi.

Picture books: There's a wealth of wonderful picture books written for older readers. They have challenging texts and picture support to aid comprehension.

Books in a series: Finding a series of books a student likes will motivate him to practice reading. A series like Horrible Harry by Suzy Kline or Magic Tree House books by Mary Pope Osborne will occupy an avid reader for months. The repetition and predictability in a series builds comprehension. Typically, each book has the same characters, so a reader can concentrate on understanding the plot.

Biographies, science, and nature books: Biographies, science, and nature books capture the imaginations of young readers. Encourage students to continue to read challenging nonfiction picture books in addition to chapter books.

71. Do you have suggestions for students who read above grade level?

Comprehension: Reading is thinking, so reading is comprehension. Once students can decode, concentrate on building comprehension skills. Meet with an advanced reader individually or, preferably, in a small group. Ask students thoughtful questions to ensure they understand what they read and are not just passing their eyes over the words. Encourage divergent thinking by asking for more than one response, such as:

"Does anyone have a different idea?"

"Yes, I know, but what if . . ."

Promote students' convergent thinking by asking questions that make them synthesize and analyze a text, such as:

"That's an interesting idea. Can you support it with facts?"

"Find evidence in the story."

Sticky notes: Encourage students to read with a pack of sticky notes. When they strongly connect to a story, have them write down their thoughts and stick their sticky note to the page where they had that thought. Sticky notes will facilitate reading-group discussions later.

Reading letters: Ask students to write a one-page letter to you each week in their reading journal. Ask them to connect their reading to their lives, to prior reading, or to the world. Respond to readers individually in a one-page letter in which you discuss your personal reading as well as what they wrote. Reading letters build strong bonds with students, and they become more careful, critical readers. This is a significant time commitment for you, but if you read a few journals each evening, it's manageable. Students in grades three and up typically read and write well enough to keep a reading journal. I have used reading journals successfully with fifth graders.

72. How can I teach vocabulary?

An effective teacher sprinkles new vocabulary into his conversations with students. You want students to be on the edge of understanding and to reach for new words. Conversely, when new vocabulary becomes part of students' spoken language, you know they understand. While children play, I listen for their acquisition of new vocabulary.

Following are some ways to help expand and improve student's vocabulary:

Read-aloud books: Read-aloud books make literature beyond students' reading level accessible. As you lead interactive read-alouds, stop frequently to ask comprehension questions and make sure students understand key vocabulary.

Reading groups: When introducing new guided reading books or basal stories to students, preteach unfamiliar words students will encounter. Check again for understanding after students have read a book.

Word games: Word games like Scrabble, Boggle, Bananagrams, and What's Gnu? teach students to make and spell new words.

Crossword puzzles: Crossword puzzles help students acquire new vocabulary. Word searches do not have the same benefit.

Writing: Writing conferences are opportunities to enrich a student's written vocabulary by suggesting alternate word choices.

Songs: Putting vocabulary to music helps students remember new words.

73. What is a word wall? How can I set up a word wall?

A word wall is a bulletin board or other wall area set aside for words. It's a reference, like a mini-dictionary for students to use as they write. Students study and are held responsible for spelling these words correctly. Words stay on a wall until students have mastered them. They'll become part of your spelling program, and you'll quiz students periodically. Tricky words, like *because*, may remain on a word wall all year.

A teacher friend told me that a local carpet store donated an area rug, which he put on his classroom wall. He attached velcro tabs to the backs of word cards and stuck them to his wall-mounted rug. Students used this word wall as one of their centers. When a student needed a word, she removed it and later returned it to the wall.

One way to introduce a word wall is to make cards with your students' first names and post them on the word wall. Spend a week learning one another's names, identifying little words within their names, and discussing vowel sounds, rhymes, etc. Then begin adding new words a few at a time. Add words students use often in their writing but can't spell, and words related to science and social studies units.

Here are a few things you'll need to create a word wall:

Alphabet cards: Use both upper- and lowercase letters. Leave spaces under letters and organize words alphabetically under the cards.

Sentence strips: Sentence strips or 3" x 5" cards for recording words.

Pointers: Have pointers nearby so students can practice reading and play interactive games with words. Pointers are especially important if your word wall is up high.

Area rug: An area rug, yards of felt, or a bulletin board for background.

74. How can I help my students develop reading fluency?

Reading fluency is reading with appropriate phrasing, inflection, and speed. By not struggling to sound out every word, a fluent reader is more apt to understand what she reads. She can comprehend because she can hold onto a thought as she reads.

A wonderful resource about fluency is *The Fluent Reader* by Timothy V. Rasinski (Scholastic, 2003). This book is full of practical suggestions and strategies you can easily implement.

Modeling: As you read aloud to students daily, you model reading fluency. The more expressively you read the better. It's important to read slowly and clearly so students understand and to stop periodically to check for listening comprehension.

Choral reading: Reading poems and rhymes aloud is one way to build fluency. While you can read picture books aloud several times, reading poetry is an easy way to work on fluency since poems are meant to be read aloud repeatedly. I've even taken the text of a picture book and written it as a poem so students could practice. Song lyrics serve the same purpose, provided students are reading as they sing.

Reader's Theater, skits, and plays: A Reader's Theater performance or play is an opportunity for repeated reading that is so painless, students won't realize they're practicing. Many books can be adapted to Reader's Theater if you scan illustrations from picture books and create PowerPoint pictures to go with the text.

> An excellent source about reading fluency is the International Reading Association (IRA) Web site: http://www.reading.org
>   There are also online activities and games at this Web site: http://www.readwritethink.org
>   To find out more about DIBELS, visit the Web site: https://dibels.uoregon.edu

Home practice: It's worth spending a few minutes at Back-to-School Night to explain reading fluency to parents, who may not be familiar with the concept. As their child's most important teachers, parents can both model and practice fluency at home. I suggest parents pick an easy book like *Green Eggs and Ham* by Dr. Seuss and read it very expressively, even over-the-top, then say to their child, "Now I want you to read this book to me the way I read it to you." A little practice every evening will contribute to a student's reading fluency. Young readers insist on reading favorite bedtime books again and again so this type of practice is natural.

Assessment: It's important to assess reading fluency at least three times a year for typical students who read on grade level or above and monthly for struggling or below-grade-level readers. I use DIBELS (Dynamic Indicators of Basic Early Literacy Skills), to assess reading fluency. Students read grade-level passages aloud and their fluency is measured in words per minute read correctly.

75. How can I guide my students so they select appropriate library books?

The better you know your students, the easier it is to help them find appropriate library books. Through interest inventories, conversation, and writing, you'll soon know who's interested in dinosaurs and who likes construction vehicles. You'll also have a sense of students' reading levels. This knowledge will guide you as you help students find library books.

It's equally important to be familiar with your school library. Spend a few after-school hours getting acquainted with your collection. Get to know your librarian and set up a weekly library check-out time.

During library check-out, students may all want your help, so you'll need to rely on library staff and teach students to select "just right" books on their own. Show your class how to use the "Five Fingers" method. Ask a student to pick a book and hold up five fingers as he reads one page. Every time he comes to a word he doesn't know, he lowers one finger. If he doesn't know five words on one page, then that book is too challenging for now. Explain that the book may be right for him in three months, but for now it will be more fun to read something else.

76. Can you recommend books to teach character and values?

The first and most important criteria in selecting books to teach character and values, or anything for that matter, is whether a book is quality literature. Well-written books with well-developed protagonists and antagonists (heroes and villains) make interesting conversations about character and values.

When a book has many characters, like Brian Jacques' *Redwall*, I separate characters into good and evil columns on chart paper, recording and discussing attributes as we read. Students have individual lists in their reading journals. Jacques' villains are awful while his heroes embody saintly qualities, so there's a marked contrast. This clear contrast is also evident in *The Chronicles of Narnia* by C.S. Lewis.

In Kate DiCamillo's *The Tale of Despereaux*, characters are more complex and nuanced. Roscuro, a rat, has both the good and bad qualities we all possess.

Equally complex is the china rabbit, Edward Tulane, in *The Miraculous Journey of Edward Tulane*, also by Kate DiCamillo. Edward is a self-centered, vain, uncaring individual who, through a series of misadventures, learns the meaning of love. This beautifully written book contains much rich material for class discussions of character and values.

For older students, *Stargirl* by Jerry Spinelli has much to teach students about conformity, courage, and being true to oneself, all appropriate values for pre-adolescents to discuss. The high school setting gives sixth graders a foretaste of what they may face in just a few years.

My favorite books, the ones I remember, are those with strong heroes and villains and stories that contrast love and hate, acceptance and rejection, good and evil, and change and intransigence.

77. Do you know of any disability-affirming books?

PICTURE BOOKS

Everybody Has Something by Margaret Dominick (disabilities)

Friends at School by Rochelle Bunnett and Matt Brown (disabilities)

Frida by Jonah Winter and Ana Juan (polio, depression)

Hooway for Wodney Wat by Helen Lester (speech disability)

Thank You, Mr. Falker by Patricia Polacco (reading disability)

CHAPTER BOOKS

Feathers by Jacqueline Woodson (hearing disability)

Hank Zipzer series by Henry Winkler (learning disabilities)

Joey Pigza Loses Control by Jack Gantos (ADHD)

Rules by Cynthia Lord (autism)

My Thirteenth Winter by Samantha Abel (anxiety)

Small Steps by Louis Sachar (cerebral palsy)

The Thing About Georgie by Lisa Graf (dwarfism)

Things Not Seen by Andrew Clements (blindness)

78. Will you suggest historical fiction and history books?

HISTORICAL FICTION	HISTORY

HISTORICAL FICTION

AVI
- Crispin: The Cross of Lead
- The Fighting Ground
- The True Confessions of Charlotte Doyle

CHRISTOPHER PAUL CURTIS
- Elijah of Buxton
- The Watsons Go to Birmingham

KAREN CUSHMAN
- Catherine, Called Birdy
- The Midwife's Apprentice

KAREN HESSE
- Brooklyn Bridge
- Letters From Rifka
- Out of the Dust
- Witness

LOIS LOWRY
- Number the Stars

ANN RINALDI (A FEW OF HER MANY TITLES):
- A Break With Charity: A Story About the Salem Witch Trials
- Cast Two Shadows: The American Revolution in the South (Great Episodes)
- The Fifth of March: A Story of the Boston Massacre (Great Episodes)
- The Secret of Sarah Revere

LAURA AMY SCHLITZ
- Good Masters! Sweet Ladies!: Voices From a Medieval Village

MILDRED D. TAYLOR
- Roll of Thunder, Hear My Cry
- Let the Circle Be Unbroken
- The Land

HISTORY

RUSSELL FREEDMAN
- Adventures of Marco Polo
- Children of the Great Depression
- Eleanor Roosevelt: A Life of Discovery
- Franklin Delano Roosevelt
- Immigrant Kids
- Indian Chiefs
- Kids at Work: Louis Hine and the Crusade Against Child Labor
- Lincoln: A Photobiography
- Who Was First?: Discovering the Americas

JIM MURPHY
- An American Plague: The True and Terrifying Story of the Yellow Fever
- Epidemic of 1793
- Blizzard!: The Storm that Changed America
- The Boys' War: Confederate and Union Soldiers Talk About the Civil War
- The Great Fire
- The Real Benedict Arnold
- A Young Patriot: The American Revolution as Experienced by One Boy

JEAN FRITZ
- And Then What Happened, Paul Revere?
- Can't You Make Them Behave, King George?
- Shh! We're Writing the Constitution
- Stonewall
- Where Do You Think You're Going, Christopher Columbus?
- Who's That Stepping on Plymouth Rock?
- Will You Sign Here, John Hancock?

79. What are your favorite children's books?

I have many favorites and continually look for new books that are unfamiliar to my students. Students can't create vivid mental images if they've seen a film version of a book, the book loses some of its power and magic.

My favorite books have themes and life lessons young students can comprehend. I select chapter books beyond the second-grade reading level so students can experience books with complex

characters and/or multiple plots. I prefer stories that feature animals as main characters because the characters communicate to children and seem real.

PICTURE BOOKS

Chrysanthemum and *Julius, the Baby of the World* by Kevin Henkes

Enemy Pie by Derek Monson

Gorky Rises, Tiffky Doofky, and *The Amazing Bone* by William Steig

Hazel's Amazing Mother and *Timothy Goes to School* by Rosemary Wells

Henry's Freedom Box by Ellen Levine

Leonardo's Horse by Jean Fritz

Much Worse Than Willy and *That Dreadful Day* by James Stevenson

CHAPTER BOOKS

Ragweed and *Poppy* from the Tales From Dimwood Forest series by Avi

The Miraculous Journey of Edward Tulane by Kate DiCamillo

The Tale of Despereaux by Kate DiCamillo

The Chronicles of Narnia series by C. S. Lewis

The Year of the Boar and Jackie Robinson by Bette Bao Lord

FOR GRADES 4–6

Five Novels by Daniel Pinkwater

Hatchet by Gary Paulsen

Harry Potter series by J. K. Rowling

Interstellar Pig by William Sleator

Number the Stars by Lois Lowry

The Treasure of Alpheus Winterborn by John Bellairs

Redwall from the Redwall series by Brian Jacques

Roll of Thunder, Hear My Cry by Mildred D. Taylor

Stargirl by Jerry Spinelli

80. How can I add books to my classroom library without spending a lot of money?

There are many inexpensive or free resources you can turn to for books to add to your classroom library:

- Garage sales
- Thrift stores
- Friends and relatives
- Wish list at school or online
- PTO and your students' parents
- Books your own children have outgrown
- Swap shop at a recycling center

81. How can I start a literature circle?

It's challenging to find time for a literature circle or book club, even one that is student-led. Several years ago, I started a book club/literature circle for second graders that met weekly during lunch. Students brought their lunch trays to our classroom, and we discussed books over lunch.

The first week I set out an array of readable chapter books and encouraged students to skim the books. Then we voted to select a book. I broke the book into manageable chunks, a few chapters each week. We didn't read during club time except to look for evidence to support an opinion. All reading was completed during independent reading or at home.

Sometimes I provided guiding questions or asked students to make up study questions for one another. I encouraged students to think divergently, to look at a story from multiple perspectives. Participants felt and acted grown-up meeting over lunch. Their questions and level of conversation were surprisingly mature. We had lively discussions and in many ways our club was like an adult book club.

82. How can I celebrate Read Across America Day?

Here's how I celebrate Read Across America Day.
I ask students to bring:

- Sleeping bag and pillow
- Water bottle and healthy snacks
- Bedroom slippers
- Stacks of books

> Read Across America Day is sponsored by National Education Association. For more information: http://www.nea.org

I push all furniture over to one side of the room and help students set up their sleeping-bag "nests" wall-to-wall. Then students read and snack all day long, stopping only for scheduled breaks and subjects like art or P.E. Students surprise themselves by reading entire pictures books or multiple chapters of chapter books. Students recall Read Across America Day as one of their favorite days. They often ask to repeat this event during the last week of school, and we do!

Grades K–3: Ask parents, teachers or administrators to stop by at intervals throughout the day to share their favorite picture book with the class.

Grades 4–6: Ask students to stop reading periodically and share their reading with classmates.

83. How can I structure independent reading time?

To set up an independent reading time, you'll need a classroom library or bookshelf and individual book boxes with appropriately leveled books for each student. Double-pocket reading folders in which students keep a list of independent reading books help students stay organized.

In September, introduce independent reading and ask students to predict and record the number of books they think they'll read during the school year. Revisit lists quarterly to revise predictions. Keep a running total of books the whole class has read, also updated quarterly, and post it outside your classroom door.

When my students return after lunch, they go immediately to book boxes or our class library and select books. Once they sit down, students may not get up, which avoids disrupting other readers.

For 15 minutes we observe a "no walking–no talking" rule. I occasionally treat the whole class to sugar-free candy while they read. Students settle down immediately and get a subliminal message that reading is sweet.

When independent reading is over, we have a "quick share" about our reading. As one student finishes a book she recommends it to a classmate rather than returning it to a shelf. This practice keeps books in circulation and promotes reading.

Writing

84. How can I set up a writing center?

A well-organized writer center should be accessible so students can use it independently. It needs to be centrally located in a cabinet, bookcase, or on a table, with baskets and bins for organizing materials.

A writing center might include:

- Many kinds of paper, including lined paper, copy paper, colored construction paper, and paper with fancy borders

- Homemade blank books

- Writing tools, including pencils, markers, colored pencils, Sharpies, pastels, and crayons

- Additional tools, like staplers, scissors, rulers, tape, correction fluid, large erasers, and glue sticks

- Basket for completed work

Be sure to teach students how to use a writing center, including such simple tasks as how to put caps on markers.

> Books about teaching writing:
>
> *Writing Through Childhood: Rethinking Process and Product* by Shelley Harwayne (Heinemann, 2001)
>
> *Writing Workshop: The Essential Guide* by Ralph Fletcher and JoAnn Portalupi (Heinemann, 2001)
>
> *How's It Going?: A Practical Guide to Conferring With Student Writers* by Carl Anderson (Heinemann, 2000)
>
> *Revisiting the Writing Workshop* by Marybeth Alley and Barbara Orehovec (Scholastic, 2007)

85. How can I get the most out of using journals?

Grades K–2: Family message journals are a great way to involve parents and children in writing. Parents encourage young children to write as families think, discuss, and write together. Students have additional opportunities to write with one-to-one guidance. Later on, students share journal entries and receive feedback when they bring their journals to school.

Before you start this project, write a letter to parents explaining message journals and your expectations. The more clearly you state what you want, the better the results. Set up a schedule for returning journals and include a calendar with your letter. Parents may need occasional reminders in your weekly newsletter.

If you expect families will not be able to write over a weekend, consider giving them a full week instead. Some families may not have time to complete school-related tasks over a weekend. This is especially true for students who visit a noncustodial parent on weekends.

Consider the type of journal families will use. Will there be space for students to draw? Will you expect students to write and draw? How much writing is enough?

Finally, think about whether you'll respond to students in writing. If you write a few sentences in response, you'll teach students that writing is two-way communication. If you collect a few journals each day, this task will be manageable.

Grades 3–6: There is a full explanation of reading response journals in *Guiding Readers and Writers Grades 3–6: Teaching Comprehension, Genre, and Content Literacy* by Irene C. Fountas and Gay Su Pinnell.

The most important part of a reading response journal are the letters between student and teacher. Students write a one-page letter every week in response to their reading. To guide student responses, give them a list of higher-level thinking questions to keep in their journals.

Then you write one-page responses to their letters. To keep this manageable, collect a few journals each day. Connect their reading to your reading. Mention books you both know and write about your own reading. Ask students questions. Through a reading response journal, you'll get to know students as readers and understand their reading challenges. A response journal also strengthens your relationships with students.

86. How can I get my primary students to write?

With young writers, I use the ideas of Lucy Calkins and encourage students to "think, draw, and write."

Writing for younger students is much more about process than product. Thinking is a first, necessary step in this process. To stimulate thinking, talk with students individually about their lives, interests, and hobbies. Offer students booklets for recording ideas or encourage them to talk through ideas as you scribe for them. When you engage in casual conversation, remind them their thoughts are potential stories. Encourage students to write in a variety of genres, including personal narrative, about topics they know or are learning about. Ask them to write in the style of their favorite authors.

> You may want to refer to a series of books to help structure Writing Workshop for young writers: *Units of Study for Primary Writing Grades K–2* by Lucy Calkins and Colleagues (Firsthand, 2005).

Next, have students sketch what they're thinking. Discuss and interpret their drawings and relate them to their thinking. Show students how adding to a drawing can expand a story.

Then, ask students to write. Scribe for those who have trouble getting started. Ask students to share their stories with classmates. Help them revise and edit based on feedback. Don't aim for perfection but do ask students to revise and edit. Remember to teach the writer, not the writing.

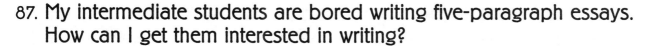

87. My intermediate students are bored writing five-paragraph essays. How can I get them interested in writing?

Blog: A class blog (Web log) or message board would likely interest your students. Find out if you have a technology teacher in your school to help with this project.

Pen pals: Find pen pals in a neighboring community or in another state or country. Encourage students to write letters. I teach at a rural school, and we had pen pals in an inner-city school about 45 minutes away. We met our pen pals at the end of the year. It was a great experience for both schools.

Letters to the Editor: Invite students to write to a local newspaper about an environmental, political, or educational issue.

Polling: Have your students take polls of other students in the school about a variety of issues and display the results using graphs.

Poetry: Take a nature walk with clipboards, pencils, and paper. Students can write poems outdoors inspired by their surroundings.

Recipes: Have students bring in a favorite cookie recipe from home. Share recipes. Vote on a favorite recipe and bake cookies. Make up an original cookie recipe.

Family stories: Ask parents and grandparents about family history. Write a story and illustrate with photos or drawings. If you have students whose ancestors immigrated via Ellis Island, you can find the ship's manifest, a photo of the ship, names and ages of those on the ship, all online. Fascinating!

Picture books: Read many picture books by one author, like William Steig. Write a story in the style of the author.

Crossword puzzles: Create crossword puzzles for one another using vocabulary from science or social studies curriculum.

Issues of equality and social justice: Fifth graders have a highly developed sense of justice and fairness. Visit the Web site of Teaching Tolerance, a project of the Southern Poverty Law Center to research an issue or event (http://www.tolerance.org). Compose a PowerPoint presentation or write a report.

Debate: This project involves speaking, reading, and writing. Have two teams take opposite sides of an issue, like global warming. Research all sides on an issue. Watch *The Great Debaters* starring Denzel Washington for more ideas. Schedule a debate and invite other classes to attend.

88. How much time should I set aside for writing? What's an effective format?

One hour per day is an adequate amount of time for writing. Here is one way to structure this time:

- Class meeting in which students discuss their plans for writing time (5 minutes)
- Mini-lesson for entire class tailored to specific needs of writers (no more than 10 minutes)
- Writing time during which students observe "no walking–no talking" rule (20–25 minutes)
- Sharing time: Everyone shares with a partner or a few writers share with the class and receive feedback—and be sure to point out any writing that ties in with mini-lesson for the day (10–15 minutes)
- Summarize and plan aloud for the following day (5 minutes)
- Clean-up time (3–5 minutes)

89. How can students publish or share their writing?

When adults think of publishing they think of books, but for students there are numerous ways to make their writing public.

- Bulletin board in hallway
- Article in class or school newsletter
- Sign in hallway, cafeteria, etc.
- Book report in library
- Pen pal letter
- Letter to editor of local paper
- Blog or message board
- Read orally to another class or grade
- Share at home with parents
- PowerPoint presentation
- Act it out as a play or skit

Social Studies, Science, and Math

90. How do you plan for celebrating special days and events?

For me, planning for special days begins with books. When I know a special day or event is coming up, I begin thinking and planning about 4–6 weeks ahead. First I skim my classroom library and select appropriate books. Then, with my librarian's help, I pick out school library books. I visit my local public library and borrow books, too.

A second and equally important source of information is the Internet. I search for video clips, read other teachers' lessons, buy more books, find art projects, and download printable activities. Most special days are already connected to history or social studies, so I make it a point to also make connections to reading, math, and science.

Once I have all the information above, I begin to plan. As I plan, I make sure to address state standards and know the concepts I will teach.

For example, the Iditarod, an Alaskan sled dog race, begins the first Saturday in March. I want students to be well-prepared before the day the race begins, so I start to plan in late January. I begin teaching in late February, so excitement will build toward the date the race begins. I keep in mind that my primary purpose in teaching the Iditarod is to meet technology standards. Using www.iditarod.com, I show second graders how to navigate a Web site.

I usually have too much material, but it's better to have too much than too little. I select just those books and activities that work with my current class. To keep units fresh, I add something new every year. This year I will add Idita-harnesses, so students can pull one another in the snow, just like the huskies pull mushers in Alaska. Adding new material and activities maintains my interest, too.

91. How can I honor cultural and ethnic heritage months?

Whether you're teaching about Black History Month, Women's History, Hispanic or Asian Heritage, here are key ideas to remember:

Study people: Studying individuals makes cultural heritage concrete and lively for students. There are multiple opportunities to teach about character and values in the lives of well-known people. It's important to research Ruby Bridges as well as Martin Luther King, Jr., and Sandra Cisneros as well as Roberto Clemente.

Honor traditions: Every group has its own traditions, whether Quinceañera or "jumping the broom." We want students to know and respect the traditions of various cultures.

Stress commonality: Understanding differences is important, but emphasize what we share.

Be fair: Be equitable in the time and energy you devote to celebrating our rich cultural and ethnic heritage. Ask different grades and classes to lead a cultural month or event so responsibility is shared and all groups are acknowledged.

Involve community: Chances are there are community members nearby who are willing share their culture with your students.

92. My colleagues and I want to plan our social studies curriculum. Can you help?

Before you plan your social studies curriculum, consult state standards for social studies. Standards are available at your state department of education Web site. If you have a district-wide or school-wide social studies curriculum, familiarize yourself with that, too. It's especially important to be in sync with state standards since students will be held accountable on statewide tests.

Here are some ways to help make social studies meaningful and memorable:

- Literature (read-alouds, take-home books, poetry, finger plays)
- Art (time lines, murals, puppets, collages, 3-D models, comics)
- Media (videos and video clips, computer software, PowerPoint presentations, Internet research, podcasts, blogs)
- Music (songs and dances, instrumental music)
- Maps and globes
- Drama (plays and skits, monologues)
- Languages (vocabulary words in other languages)
- Costumes (dress-up, biography reports)
- Food and cooking
- Celebrations (celebrate holidays from other cultures)
- Field trips
- Activities that include Parents (family history, careers)
- Games

93. What can I do to spice up my social studies program?

The human brain seeks novelty, so ask thought-provoking questions throughout a lesson. Questions should gradually build toward a central point. Consider ways to group students to promote discussion. Students as young as first grade can be asked to think about a question, find a partner, and share. This is referred to as, "Think, pair, share."

Small discussion or research groups work well for students in Grade 2 and up. Primary students lack advanced social skills but can maintain themselves as group members for short periods of time. Upper elementary students can work cooperatively for two to three weeks.

Visuals are important to support discussion and maintain student focus. Many students are visual learners and need visual support to enhance comprehension. An overhead projector, SmartBoard, or laptop with projector will add to your lessons. Maps, time lines, Venn diagrams, and tables also amplify discussion.

Additional strategies:

Role-plays: Role-plays are short, spontaneous acting challenges. To organize for role-plays plan the scenarios and individuals to be portrayed in advance and write them on 3" x 5" cards. Then, when you have a few minutes at the beginning or end of class, draw a card.

Read-aloud plays: Scholastic has books of historical plays that don't require costumes or props.

Music: Music promotes understanding of history and culture.

Cultural events: If you study China, celebrate the Chinese New Year. If you study Mexico, celebrate El Dia de las Muertos or Las Posadas.

Monuments and symbols: Students relate to symbols and monuments. When my students study immigration, they find out about the history of the Statue of Liberty and Ellis Island. When they study China, they learn about China's Great Wall and the Terra Cotta Warriors of X'ian.

94. Do you have suggestions for social studies centers?

Geography center: You'll need atlases, a wall map, compasses, and a globe. A geography question on a sentence strip can be changed weekly.

Create-a-map center: Simple outline maps, colored pencils, and Sharpies are all that's needed for this center. Map of the Month Club is a good source for large, desktop-sized outline maps.

Computers: Google Earth enables students to travel the world, from their own backyards to the Eiffel Tower and the Great Wall of China.

Listening center: Historical fiction or history book on CD/tape.

Writing center: Students can write letters to historical figures asking them questions. Other students can select one of the letters and answer from the historical figure's point of view.

Art center: There are countless possibilities for an art center. A couple of ideas include making quill pens or cross-stitch samplers during a Colonial America unit, recreating a Chinese compass or painting drums during a unit on China.

95. How can I make science more interesting and engaging?

Biological supply house: Order specimens for dissection from a biological supply house such as Carolina Biological Supply (http://www.carolina.com). Two specimens I've used are owl pellets and dogfish shark. With owl pellets, I demonstrate a dissection first and then let students explore owl pellets with lab partners. Since I can only afford one shark, I dissect while students observe. Students write lab reports and draw diagrams of their observations.

Space-age ant farm: There's an ant farm filled with clear blue gel rather than soil. (You can find it at http://www.thinkgeek.com.) It's like an ant farm NASA used to send ants into space. The gel contains all the nutrients and water that ants need. Observe the colony and the web of interconnected tunnels as ants dig. Ants live about three weeks, so there's plenty of time for observations.

Technology: Digital Blue is a microscope connected to a monitor or laptop. Students can create slideshows, video clips, and even add music. (See Digital Blue Microscope at http://www.digiblue.com.)

Web sites: There are wonderful science and nature Web sites including those for National Geographic, San Francisco Exploratorium, and Journey North, a site about animal migration.

96. Can you help me plan lessons for an economics unit?

K–1: Create a pretend store in housekeeping area. Students buy and sell plastic food with play money. Change the store occasionally. Make it a pet store that sells stuffed animals, a hardware store that sells nails and screws, or a restaurant with menus and order slips.

Grades 1–6: A bake sale is a great way to teach economics. Students learn about planning, forecasting, advertising, sales, and banking. They learn about supply and demand. Planning a bake sale takes time and the participation of all of your students and their parents.

Grades 5–6: Federal Reserve Bank of Boston (http://www.bos.frb.org/education/index.htm) is a resource for teaching economics. They have developed computer-based interactive units targeted at middle school students.

97. How can I help my students learn the math facts?

Automatic recall of addition/subtraction and multiplication/division facts is important to free a student's mind to solve problems.

Here are some ways to practice:

Flash cards: Make flash cards on 3″ x 5″ cards. Write the more difficult sums like 9 + 7 = 16. Since students need to find sums vertically and horizontally, show both ways. Punch a hole in one corner of each card and put the cards on a metal ring. As students master their sums, cards are removed and other more challenging sums replace them. There are Web sites where students can create and print flash cards.

Parent involvement: One key to mastering math facts is parent involvement. Students must practice at home because there's not enough time in the school day for students to learn math facts.

Mad Minutes: Short, daily timed tests of addition/subtraction and multiplication/division facts. The ultimate goal is to solve 40 facts in one minute.

Computer programs: Programs like Scholastic's FASTTMath are effective when used daily for 15 minutes.

Web sites: There are many Web-based games. Math Playground, for example, has a timed game in which a student plays against herself and solves as many problems as she can within one minute.

The National Library of Virtual Manipulatives is also a useful resource.

Number line and one hundred chart: It's important for primary grade students to memorize and internalize a number line and one hundred chart so they can picture it and move numbers around in their head.

> The following Web sites include helpful information:
> AAA Math:
> http://www.aaamath.com
> MathSphere (for board games):
> http://www.mathsphere.co.uk/resources
> Math Playground:
> http://www.mathplayground.com
> Math Is Fun
> http://www.mathsisfun.com
> National Library of Virtual Manipulatives
> http://nlvm.usu.edu

98. How can I organize and teach a math problem of the day?

A well-organized problem of the day is a brain warm-up that lasts about ten minutes. There's no one right way to teach problem of the day.

My problem of the day is waiting on an overhead projector when students arrive. Once students have written and labeled their answers, we discuss the problem. To encourage divergent thinking, students explain their thinking and show the equations they used to solve the problem. Students learn there's more than one strategy for solving problems.

Reaching All Learners

99. How can I provide differentiated instruction?

Differentiated homework: One way to differentiate is to provide homework on a variety of levels. This works especially well for math and reading. It takes a little additional planning time but it's workable and meets individual needs.

Elephant Words spelling: Elephant Words is an easy way to differentiate spelling. Students who do well on Monday's grade-level spelling pretests may substitute words of their choice for Friday's post-test. Encourage students to select words in categories like states, countries, sports, animals, fruits and vegetables, etc. Students take more ownership when they select their own words. I test all students on Friday. Although this takes a few minutes of class time, those with Elephant Words inspire other students to study.

> This is just one of many books by Carol Ann Tomlinson, leading writer about differentiation:
> *The Differentiated Classroom: Responding to the Needs of All Learners* by Carol Ann Tomlinson (ASCD, 1999).

After-school program: An after-school enrichment program in science, math, or chess is one way to differentiate.

All-school unit: An all-school program in the arts with a school-wide performance or exhibit as a culminating activity appeals to many students' strengths.

Teach to individuals and small groups: Meeting with small groups for reading and math instruction and for literature circles is another way to differentiate.

100. How can I plan an enrichment program for my class? For my school?

For your class, keep it simple. As you get to know your students' strengths, you'll find ways to extend the curriculum and challenge them.

Address multiple intelligences: Consider multiple intelligences as you plan for different kinds of learners.

Include the arts: Find ways to integrate music, dance, and visual arts into your curriculum.

Ask parents: If you ask, parents may volunteer to plan enriching activities like field trips.

Form a club: At school, a club program works well either in after-school or as a Friday afternoon activity. A school-wide enrichment program is a big commitment that will likely include parents and community members, as well as teachers and administrators.

Let students select from a list of clubs that adults are prepared to lead. Gear clubs to adult talents, student interests, and multiple intelligences. Consider clubs like Hip-Hop Dance, School News Show, Basketball, and Computers.

Here are two clubs that might interest students:

Math Club: Students solve cool problems in geometry, graphing, statistics, and probability. Use math Web sites, and online problems of the week. Play math and logic games like checkers, Mancala, and Connect Four. This is supposed to be fun, but increasing practice with higher-level thinking does improve test scores.

> Mindware is also a great source for games and activities that promote higher level thinking: http://www.mindwareonline.com/MWEstore/Home/HomePage.aspx?

Chess Club: You'll need chess sets and computer software like Scholastic's fabulous CD, Chessmaster. Chessmaster Academy (on CD) has short lessons. Students watch a lesson or two each week and then play. Since chess doesn't involve reading, this club works for grades 2–6. I've had a chess club for the past three years. Although I hadn't played chess before, I learned along with the kids.

101. How can I help an English language learner fit in socially with English-speaking classmates?

It takes time for English-speaking students to adjust to a new school. This adjustment process is longer and more complicated for ELL students.

Be positive: Your smiling face and acceptance will help your new student relax. Her classmates, who take their cues from you, will sense and adopt your positive attitude. Regardless of what you feel, act like your new student's presence is a joy, not a burden.

One of your responsibilities as a classroom teacher is to include all students in your class community. It's up to you to help her find a place among her classmates.

Assign buddies: Find two patient, mature students to partner with this student in class and cafeteria, and on the bus and playground. Two buddies can take turns and support one another as they include their new classmate. It's not necessary for the buddies to speak the ELL student's first language. After two weeks, pass this responsibility on to two other students.

Celebrate culture: Find out about your new student's native country and share what you learn with your class. Learn a few words in her first language.

Be vigilant: Despite your best efforts, this student may be victimized by bullies who prey on vulnerable children. Be aware of any teasing, mimicking, and bullying and address any problems promptly.

Include parents: Although your new student's parents may not speak English, reach out to them. If you see them at school or in the community, smile and introduce yourself. If they visit school, make them welcome.

102. How can I structure academics for an English language learner?

Your school may have ELL tutors who will work with your ELL student several hours a week, but much of his school day will be spent with you and his classmates. As with all students, look for academic and social strengths to capitalize on. Strategies that are beneficial for ELL students will benefit English-speaking classmates as well.

Visuals: At first this student will learn primarily visually. Increase the number of visuals you use in your teaching. Use overhead and LED projectors, an interactive whiteboard, PowerPoint slides, charts, posters, and graphs.

Make it concrete: Plan more hands-on activities in science and social studies. Play board games and playground games that are not language-dependent.

Instructions: Explain oral and written instructions one-on-one. Make up samples of crafts and projects so student can see an end product before beginning work.

Math: Math computation may be an area of strength. Observe an ELL student during math class for signs he is following along. Use manipulatives.

Tone of voice: Use your voice as you would with English-speaking students.

103. Can you put together a Spanish/English bilingual book list for my students?

All the books on this list are available in both English and Spanish. When you teach reading with one of these books, offer the Spanish edition to those students who are more comfortable and confident in Spanish. If you speak Spanish, you might occasionally read an important passage or chapter in both English and Spanish. I have included picture books because they are more accessible than chapter books for English language learners.

PICTURE BOOKS
- *Diego* by Jonah Winter (biography of Diego Rivera)
- *Frida* by Jonah Winter (biography of Frida Kahlo)
- *Doctor Desoto* by William Steig
- *Verdi* by Janell Cannon
- *Jumanji* by Chris Van Allsburg
- *Princess Smartypants* by Babette Cole
- *Pecos Bill* by Steven Kellogg
- *Paul Bunyan* by Steven Kellogg

SERIES
- *Josefina – An American Girl* by Valerie Tripp from the American Girl Collection
- *Tut Tut* by Jon Scieszka from the Time Warp Trio series
- *A Series of Unfortunate Events* by Lemony Snicket

CHAPTER BOOKS
- *Eragon* by Christopher Paolini
- *Eldest* by Christopher Paolini
- *Esperanza Rising* by Pam Muñoz Ryan
- *Baseball in April* by Gary Soto
- *Danny, the Champion of the World* by Roald Dahl
- *Silverwing* by Kenneth Oppel

AMERICAN HISTORY
- *Where are you going, Christopher Columbus?* by Jean Fritz
- *Chasing Redbird* by Sharon Creech
- *Lyddie* by Katherine Paterson
- *Amos Fortune, Free Man* by Elisabeth Yates
- *Roll of Thunder, Hear My Cry* by Mildred D. Taylor

CHAPTER VI

BEYOND THE CLASSROOM

Starting Your Career

104. How can I find a teaching job?

Stay positive and project self-confidence. Try to get out and meet people. The more educators and administrators you meet, the greater your chances for employment. Remember, jobs do become available at the last minute. Consider these questions and ideas when job hunting:

- Do you live near where you grew up? Have you applied to the school district you attended as a student? Networking with former teachers works.

- Have you hand-delivered your resume to schools? Call a principal and tell him you'd like to stop by with your resume even if he has no openings.

- Stay flexible about where you will work. Consider a job in a nearby city, especially if public transportation is available. Think broadly and don't limit yourself.

- Consider relocating. States experiencing rapid growth do have openings.

- If you are new to a community, join a newcomers club and volunteer at a school. The more teachers and community members who know you, the better.

- Consider a teaching-related job for one year. Working as a substitute, assistant, individual assistant, before- and/or after-school leader, YMCA, Boys or Girls Club leader, or tutor will give you a chance to show your skills and gain experience.

> To find specific, targeted openings, search a school district's Web site for employment opportunities. Here are two Web sites I've used:
> http://www.schoolspring.com
> http://www.topschooljobs.org
> (from the education periodical, *Education Week*)
>
> Both sites allow you to narrow your search and include national and international job opportunities for teachers and administrators.

105. Do I need a master's degree?

A master's degree is an investment that will pay for itself in a few years. Having a master's degree may open other career possibilities in leadership or administration. There are many benefits, including the knowledge you'll gain, the networking you'll do with professors and other teachers, and an increase in salary when you jump onto a master's salary scale. Some states require that teachers have a master's degree within five years. Check the requirements at your state department of education Web site.

106. How can I prepare for job interviews?

As with any position, it's important to be prepared for a job interview. Start by researching your school on the Internet. Be familiar with the size, demographics, and standardized test scores. Check the Web site for photos of the principal and staff and become familiar with their names and faces. Talk to

community members you know about the school. Try to get a sense of its strengths and weaknesses.

Wear a suit to add to your professional demeanor. Arrive ten minutes early and bring a portfolio of materials from your student teaching or previous teaching experience. Be sure to thank the interviewers before and after your interview. You may want to send a follow-up note or e-mail.

Here are questions you might be asked:

- Why do you want to teach? Why do you want to teach at our school?

- What are your greatest strengths and weaknesses as a teacher? How do you plan to address your weaknesses?

- How will you create a classroom community with a group of diverse learners from different racial, ethnic, and/or socioeconomic backgrounds?

- What is project-based learning? Can you give an example?

- If you worked with a student reading two years below grade level who was not receiving special education services, how would you get help? How would you accommodate this student in your classroom?

- What is the difference between formative and summative assessments? Give examples of each. Which type of assessment is more valuable to teachers? Students?

- How do you introduce students to a new book? Can you give an example?

- How will you include special education and English language learners?

- What areas of math do you especially enjoy teaching? How will you use manipulatives to enhance math instruction?

- What books have you read lately? What authors and genres do you enjoy?

- What do you do in your free time? How do you manage stress and maintain balance in your life?

107. What questions should I ask at my job interview?

Interviewing for a job is a two-way street, so make sure you have an opportunity to ask questions. Time is usually set aside for your questions at the end of an interview. If no one asks, it's appropriate to say, "I have a few questions I'd like to ask."

Confirm the level of support you can expect as a new teacher in their school. And make sure you leave the interview with an understanding of what will be expected of you.

Here are questions you might ask:

- What kind of orientation program or support group do you have for new teachers?

- How many hours are devoted to teacher orientation?

- Who will be my mentor teacher? How often will we meet?

- In what ways am I responsible to my mentor teacher?

- What is your process for supervising and evaluating teachers?

- What are the hours I'm expected to be in the building?

- What is your dress code?

- Do you have a policy handbook for teachers? May I have a copy?

- Is there anything else you'd like to ask me?

108. How can I decide if the job I've been offered is right for me?

When deciding whether or not to accept a job offer, consider more than salary and benefits. Every school is unique and has a distinctive culture and style. Taking a tour and meeting administrators and teachers will give you a snapshot of a school's culture. If you can, contact parents, students, or community members and chat with them as well. Drive or walk around the school's immediate neighborhood. Safety and security are issues in some communities, so make sure you feel safe. Search a local newspaper's Web site for recent news articles. You may learn about challenging issues a school is facing, like low test scores or a tight budget.

Consider saying "yes" even if you have to compromise on grade level. The grade level you teach is less important than other factors. Once you have a position in a given school, you may transition within a year or two to the grade you initially wanted.

It's a good idea to make a list of pros and cons and discuss your list with family and friends. Remember to weigh other job offers in the balance. Finally, trust your intuition.

Working With Colleagues and Administrators

109. What are the most common concerns about new teachers?

Commitment: Teaching is a profession that demands a high level of personal commitment. A teacher who is committed to a school's mission, students, and colleagues is valued.

Control and consistency: One concern among coworkers is whether a new teacher will be able to control her class. Other teachers observe a new teacher's class as students pass by classroom doors or play on the playground. Consistency in a new teacher's enforcement of rules and her students' respect for her authority are noted by other teachers and administrators. Consistency is also the ability to get quality work from all students for an entire school year.

Competence: There is no substitute for deep knowledge about subjects a teacher will teach. Another aspect of competence is being well-organized and managing a classroom effectively.

Communication: Good interpersonal skills and an ability to build relationships are essential for teachers. It's especially important to be able to talk with parents and work effectively with them on their child's behalf. The ability to write coherent, well-organized notes, e-mails, and reports is needed. A new teacher has to speak up when things go wrong and ask for help as needed.

Collaboration: A willingness to work cooperatively as a team member is admired by colleagues and administrators. Sharing ideas with others and requesting feedback are aspects of collaboration.

110. What big challenges do new teachers face?

The biggest challenges new teachers face are in three key areas: support, discipline, and classroom management. These questions will help you focus your efforts to overcome the challenges:

SUPPORT
- Is there a new teacher orientation program?
- Are school policies and procedures in writing for new teachers?
- Does a new teacher have an assigned mentor teacher? Do they meet weekly?
- Does a new teacher's administrator check in with her frequently?
- Are colleagues available weekly for team or grade-level meetings?
- Do teachers plan together or assist a new teacher with planning?

DISCIPLINE

- Are a new teacher's students respectful toward one another and their teacher?
- Does she have rules in place that she reinforces?
- Are there logical consequences for students who don't follow the rules?
- Does a new teacher's class move around the building in an orderly way?
- Does she know how to handle difficult students and situations? Does she know when to ask for support?

CLASSROOM MANAGEMENT

- Is a new teacher well-organized? Does he follow a schedule?
- Are systems in place that make the school day run smoothly?
- Does a new teacher work effectively with assistants and other adults in the classroom?
- Is time used effectively? Is pacing appropriate for a given class?
- Does a new teacher advocate for his students?
- Is a new teacher sensitive to diverse learners?
- Are all students treated fairly without regard for race, gender, socioeconomic status, etc.?
- Is a new teacher able to multitask?

111. I am young and inexperienced. How can I earn my colleagues' trust and respect?

The best way to earn your colleagues' respect is through hard work. Arrive early and stay late. Keep your room neat and organized. Change your bulletin boards monthly and use them as opportunities to display your students' best work.

Express your love for teaching. Add your own unique contributions to the curriculum.

Show colleagues you're motivated and interested in gaining skills. Ask questions and consult with them when you have difficult situations. Try to learn at least one thing from every teacher you meet.

Volunteer to serve on committees. Experienced teachers have worked on committees for years and would likely welcome your ideas. They will get to know you better, and you will build relationships with them.

Ask about their hobbies and families. Once in a while, bring donuts or chocolate chip cookies (or carrot and celery sticks, along with a dip that doesn't require refrigeration) leave in the faculty room.

112. What kind of support can I expect from my mentor teacher and how can I get the most out of her expertise?

At your job interview or shortly thereafter, you want to establish the kind of support you can expect from your mentor. Mentor teachers are usually paid a stipend for their services. They've been specially trained to assist new teachers and have accepted the added responsibility and time commitment.

It is reasonable to expect your mentor to work with you at a regularly scheduled weekly meeting of about 30 minutes. Weekly meetings are opportunities to debrief the past week and discuss your plans for the coming week. In addition, you can expect your mentor to be available during the week in the event you have a teaching emergency.

Remember to advocate for yourself. If your mentor is not living up to your expectations, contact an administrator right away.

To get the most out of your mentor's expertise, be sure to:

Take the initiative: Approach your mentor teacher first. Tell her how much you're looking forward to getting together and suggest several times including lunchtime, when you might meet. Tell her you'll bring brownies. Keep your invitation short and upbeat.

Schedule meetings in advance: At your first meeting, tell your mentor you'd like to meet with her once a week for 30 minutes for the first 12 weeks of school and then assess your needs. Assure her that you are working towards independence but want to tap into her experience and expertise.

Written agenda: A weekly meeting of 30 minutes is appropriate and enough time to mentor you if you use time wisely. Prepare a written agenda for your meetings and bring a prioritized list of questions in writing. Be organized and move the meeting along so get your questions answered. Keep meetings to 30 minutes. Thank her for her time at the end of each meeting.

Consult colleagues: If you need additional help between meetings, ask coworkers or team members. They may be able to give you more specific advice.

Give mentor thinking time: Don't expect immediate solutions to all your problems. As a mentor teacher, I know mentors need time to sort out what's happening and generate ideas and solutions.

113. Why isn't my principal more helpful?

Make an appointment: Be proactive. Make an appointment with your principal. Prepare for your meeting by making a prioritized list of your questions and concerns. Practice at home what you'll say at the meeting.

When you meet, thank your principal for meeting with you and ask for suggestions about how you can become a more effective teacher. Listen carefully and take notes. Don't be defensive, just concentrate on listening. You'll probably gain new understanding and insight from this meeting.

Principal's perspective: Look at your situation from a principal's perspective. Your principal, who wears numerous hats, may have several new teachers in his school, some of whom are more needy than you. He has to ration his time with any one teacher in order to visit all classrooms and supervise and evaluate all teachers.

Mentor teacher: If you have a mentor teacher, contact her and arrange a meeting. She may be able to give you concrete suggestions that will make a difference in your working relationship with the principal.

> To view your situation from a principal's perspective, go to the Web site of the Association for Supervision and Curriculum Development:
> http://www.ascd.org
> You may want to check out their books and *Educational Leadership* magazine.
>
> For another source of information with an administrator's point of view, look at *Education Week*, in print or the Web:
> http://www.edweek.org

School culture: Every school has its own unique atmosphere, customs, and rituals. Perhaps it's part of your school culture that teachers don't ask the principal for help. Talk with veteran teachers to uncover hidden attitudes about administrators at your school.

Right fit: Although you may work in a fabulous school with skillful colleagues and eager students, this may not be the right school for you. By March, if you are still unhappy, consider applying for teaching jobs at other schools in your area. Life is too short to be miserable.

114. My principal is treating me unfairly. What can I do?

Document: Document all conversations in writing as soon as possible after they occur. From now on, it's best if requests for assistance and other communication with your principal be in writing. Save all documents, including e-mails. This builds a paper trail.

Inform union: Are you a union member? If you are, contact the union representative in your building. Present the facts to your rep and ask for help. Especially if you have tenure, your union can help you. Your union rep may refer you to a union lawyer for advice.

Record teaching plans and strategies: Keep careful classroom records. Write your weekly plans in detail. List strategies you try with your class. For each strategy, write how long you try it and how effectively it works. Continue to add to this list.

Assessments: Do you assess student progress regularly? Do you give both pretests and post-tests? Keep copies of all tests and other assessments. Assessment results showing growth over time demonstrate that you are an effective teacher.

Take care of yourself: Keep balance in your life by exercising regularly and getting plenty of rest. Find a friend, not a colleague, who will listen to you "vent." Seek outside counseling. Just talking about a difficult situation helps.

115. My principal wants me to be friendlier. How can I improve?

There may be several reasons your principal says you're unfriendly. Here are strategies that will make you appear friendlier.

Smile!: Sometimes we're so preoccupied multitasking we appear more serious than we feel. We forget to smile at our students. Get a joke book or humorous picture book and lighten everyone's day with humor. Laugh at your own mistakes. Regardless of what you're feeling, turn up the corners of your mouth, and you'll instantly relax. When you smile more, you enjoy teaching more. Try it, it works!

Listen and empathize: You may not agree with what a student or parent says, but listen carefully without interrupting or defending. Then express empathy for them and their position. Smile and nod as appropriate. Wait 30 seconds after they stop talking before you speak. If you don't have time to conference with a parent or student on the spot, schedule an appointment to discuss their issue.

Body language: We send unconscious nonverbal signals about our mood through body language. Try sitting occasionally if you're standing all day. Sitting not only allows you time to relax, it tells your students you're willing to share power with them. When talking to young students, sit or kneel so you're on their level and maintain eye contact. Decrease the distance you are standing from others. This is easy to do and subtly affects others' perception of you.

Praise: Use praise liberally but genuinely. Praise students so they feel safe and relaxed. Praise parents for their children and parenting skills. Praise colleagues for their lessons and bulletin boards. Ask them about their spouses and children. Promise yourself you won't say anything negative about your colleagues or school for three weeks.

116. Instead of complaining to me, a parent went over my head to my principal. What can I do?

There's not much you can do about this particular situation. Make an appointment to see your principal and tell her you wish parents would come to you first. Ask about her view on the appropriate chain of command. Assuming your principal wants parents to come to you first, you need to explain this school policy to parents.

Parent Night: At Parent Night or Back-to-School Night, tell parents how to reach you. Give them your e-mail address and your school phone number. (You may also choose to provide your home number, but *not* your cell phone number.) Tell them when you're available to conference with them, for instance, before and after school or during planning time.

Weekly newsletter: Mention several times in your weekly newsletter that you hope parents will contact you directly if they have a question, concern, or idea for you. (Don't use the words problem or suggestion.) Inform parents it's school policy to contact you first before calling your principal.

Stand by your classroom door: Once a week before school, stand by your door or on the playground, wherever you're likely to see parents. Parents may engage you in conversation, and you may clear up questions and misunderstandings on the spot.

Be proactive: At Parent Night, ask parents repeatedly during your presentation if they have questions. You want them to leave feeling all their questions were answered.

> To understand more about parents' perspective, visit the PTO Web site: http://www.ptotoday.com

If a student has an isolated academic or social problem at school, write a brief note to his parents the same day and slip it into the student's homework folder.

If a student has chronic problems, call her parents promptly and arrange a conference. It's much easier to take the initiative and deal with problems proactively.

117. Why does my principal side with angry parents instead of supporting me?

There are a variety of reasons why a principal may side with parents.

- Sometimes a principal sides with parents because it's easier. He has less control in his relationships with parents than his relationships with subordinates. He may be confident you'll bounce back from this incident, but concerned these angry parents may not.

- A principal has to work with parents for several years, so he has a long-term perspective on his relationships with parents. He may extend himself and compromise to maintain open communication with difficult parents.

- Principals want parents to feel their point of view is represented. He may feel you represent the school's perspective while he represents parents. This may happen at your expense.

- Your principal may be shielding you from further conflict. For example, if you and a parent had a conflict of values about respect, quality work, effort, etc., it's unlikely there will be a meeting of the minds. When a conflict of values occurs, it may be best to let your principal handle it.

- What I've realized, at times the hard way, is I can't solve all problems. I can't fix every angry parent, nor should I be expected to do so. Knowing when to let go and let a principal handle a difficult situation is part of growing as a teacher.

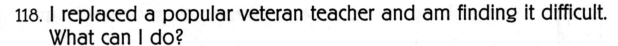

118. I replaced a popular veteran teacher and am finding it difficult. What can I do?

When your new students whine, "But that's not how Mrs. Smith did it," they're demonstrating loyalty to their former teacher. On some level, they're angry about Mrs. Smith's departure and think it's okay to disrespect you. They also know if they talk about Mrs. Smith, they'll frustrate you. You may think your students don't know what you're feeling, but they probably know you're upset and may purposely "push your buttons" to get a reaction. Hide your exasperation. Breathe deeply and keep your composure. It is important not to let students know you're upset.

Practice at home in front of a mirror what you'll say in response to, "But that's not how Mrs. Smith did it." Engage in positive self-talk. Stick to your methods, because you know what works for you. You don't have to teach like Mrs. Smith to be an effective teacher. Students can learn from many kinds of teachers. Being able to learn from different people is an essential life skill.

With regard to parents, keep them informed through your weekly newsletter. Tell them your planned activities. Parents want to know you're self-confident and have a game plan. They'll find it easier to let go of Mrs. Smith than their children.

It's difficult to retire and give up a 35-year career, especially for a popular teacher. You might contact Mrs. Smith once in a while and ask her a question or two. This will make her feel valued and included and ease her feelings of loneliness.

119. What is it like to replace a teacher on maternity leave?

When a teacher takes maternity leave, she knows well in advance when she'll need a replacement. A long-term substitute teacher is hired to fill in for a few months to one year.

You know up-front this assignment is time-limited. If you have only a few months to spend with a class, continue the routines and procedures established and/or recommended by their teacher. If you choose to make changes, proceed slowly.

This long-term assignment is a chance for you to impress the principal and your coteachers with your classroom management and organizational skills. With hard work, you can leverage this job into a permanent teaching position in your school or district.

Students may talk openly about missing their former teacher and unfavorably compare you to her. Be tolerant and understanding. It may bolster your students and your standing among them if you invite their teacher to visit with her new baby.

120. I am returning from maternity leave at midyear. How can I make my new life work?

Since you'll return at midyear, arrange to spend a day or two observing your class with the current teacher. Sit in the back of the room and help out a little. Observe routines and procedures that are in place. Observing will allow you time to transition back to teaching full-time. Set aside several hours when students aren't present to chat with your substitute so he can bring you up to date on your students. You may observe students you want to ask him about.

For the first month, follow established routines and do what the current teacher has been doing. Don't make changes immediately. Instead, give students a chance to get acquainted with you. Just your presence will be enough change. They'll have loyalty to their previous teacher, so complimenting him

in their presence and continuing to say nice things about him after he's gone will help your students adjust. Besides, you want to go easy on yourself. You're coming back from maternity leave and may not be sleeping through the night. So take it easy and keep it simple. At home, enjoy your baby and the time you have together. Make time for yourself to rest and exercise. Go to bed early rather than grading all those papers. Paperwork can wait.

121. How can I manage a classroom assistant?

An assistant works under a teacher's direction. She may not be a trained teacher, but even if she is a certified teacher, her job is to assist you. Working with an assistant requires patience on your part because you have to train your assistant.

It takes time to build a positive working relationship with a classroom assistant. If you are a young teacher, working with a mature assistant who is established in a school can be nervewracking.

Overall, be assertive but kind. Maintain a professional relationship with your assistant. Don't confide in her or gossip about colleagues. She is not your mom or friend; she is your helper. Set boundaries and keep a professional distance. However, I do make a point to acknowledge my assistant with a card and gift on her birthday and at the end of the year.

Responsibilities of assistants typically fall into two categories: clerical and teaching support.

Clerical: Recording lunch count and attendance, copying, laminating, and readying materials are a few of an assistant's clerical duties. A well-trained assistant knows what her teacher needs and does these jobs without being asked. Set aside a bin or basket for documents you want copied. This "to-do" basket will keep your assistant occupied when she has spare time.

Teaching support: Classroom assistants also work with students. While they don't plan lessons, assistants do carry out lessons planned by teachers. An assistant might help a struggling student, assist in a computer lab with software and the Internet, transcribe a story, give a spelling test, and/or supervise students on the playground and in the cafeteria.

Develop an hour-by-hour daily schedule for your assistant, with tasks carefully enumerated. A written schedule clearly shows you expect her to work throughout the day. At the beginning of the year, work with your assistant during your planning periods to ensure she knows how to do what you're asking of her.

Set aside about five minutes at the beginning of each day to tell your assistant what's planned and answer her questions. At the end of the day, quickly debrief the day's events.

Here are some other responsibilities you can delegate to an assistant:
- Hang up hats and coats
- Straighten cubbies
- Answer parents' questions while you start your day
- Keep track of bus notes and early dismissals
- Give you notes from parents promptly
- Empty and fill homework folders and record homework
- Fill student mailboxes
- Teach one-to-one reading program
- Put up and take down bulletin boards
- Help high-need students
- Assist at library checkout
- Arrange field trips
- Prepare and lead art projects
- Run errands with students
- Fill in for you while you are at a meeting
- Help students at dismissal

122. How can I work with colleagues to support a student with emotional needs?

First steps: Start by chatting with your school psychologist or guidance counselor, who may offer support. Your psychologist may share what she knows about this student, her school history, and family life. Ask about strategies that have worked in the past. In particular, ask about behavior modification. Find out if this student is receiving counseling in school and/or in the community. Observe the student on the playground and in the classroom and cafeteria. Take notes. Show your notes to the psychologist and ask her to come and observe this student in class.

Child study team: Many schools have a problem-solving team that consists of a special educator, psychologist, occupational therapist, speech and language pathologist, principal, parents, and classroom teacher. When a student is at risk, a teacher or specialist can call a meeting to discuss the student and come up with appropriate strategies. Ask your administrator.

Evaluation: Once interventions suggested by the Child Study Team are implemented, wait to determine if they have the desired effect. If not, the team meets again and an evaluation is considered. Ask for a psychological evaluation and perhaps an educational evaluation if the student has academic difficulties. Possibly request evaluations from speech and language and occupational therapists. Later meet to discuss evaluation results and recommend actions for the future. Test results may indicate this student needs an Individual Education Plan (IEP).

List of high-risk students: Our psychologist makes a list of all emotionally at-risk students and divides up the students among our faculty and staff. Every adult says "hi" and checks in daily with one or two at-risk students. Every staff member knows the names of all at-risk students, and we work together to strengthen their connections to caring adults.

Working With Parents

123. How can I structure parent conferences?

The following approach has been effective for me in structuring parent conferences:

Organize in advance: I prepare a conference form, which I create myself. On my form there's space to record results of all assessments including DIBELS Test of Reading Fluency, spelling test of top 100 high-frequency words, math readiness test, math chapter tests, and timed test of addition and subtraction facts. It also includes student's reading group and reading level, a record of absences and late arrivals, a short blurb about social and emotional growth, and a few lines for additional notes. I complete this form for each student and make a copy for parents to take home. This is especially helpful when only one parent attends a conference. I speak from the form, which helps me focus on facts. As a rule, I don't take notes during a parent conference because I've found it makes parents anxious.

On conference day: I have number lines, 100 charts, alphabets, and book lists available for parents to take home to assist with homework. I also have on hand student work samples, texts, and folders to refer to as needed. I put chairs in the hall so parents will have a place to sit while they wait. There are fresh bulletin boards to entertain them, as well as a three-ring binder full of class stories.

Informal meeting spot: I meet with parents at a round table, rather than across a desk because it sets a friendly, open tone. Some parents had negative experiences when they were students, for other parents English is not their native language. So I'm sensitive to the possibility parents may feel nervous about meeting with me to discuss their child's progress.

I shake hands with parents as I greet them and maintain eye contact with parents throughout the conference. The more I smile and present a relaxed demeanor, the more parents relax.

First ask, then tell: I begin a conference with small talk about their child. Every child has relative strengths, and I bring up strengths first. Then I ask parents if they have any questions. Parents may come to a conference with an agenda, so I address their questions and concerns proactively. Even when parents don't have questions, I let them know they can ask questions any time during our meeting. One of my goals is to make sure their questions are answered.

Share the facts: After a few minutes, as parents feel relaxed and comfortable, I discuss assessment results in the context of goals students typically achieve. I tell parents that students grow a lot in one academic year and make significant academic progress, as I refer to the facts. Focusing on facts keeps me on-message and prevents talking about my impressions.

Tell the truth: It's important to tell parents the truth, directly and diplomatically. Parents know I'm honest. I speak slowly, clearly, and directly, and I try to be diplomatic, too. Parents of younger students may have difficulty hearing what their child's teacher is saying. This may be the first time they have heard the truth, so my goal is to convey little bits of truth in ways parents can receive them. This can be tricky, especially when a student has a disability or pronounced area of weakness.

Parents may ask for help with parenting, medical, or emotional/behavioral issues. When parents bring up topics beyond teaching and learning, I explain I'm not an expert in that area, but I'd be happy to refer them to someone else. It's important to know names of specialists and resources in your particular school and district in case parents need additional help.

Summarize: At the end of the conference, I summarize our meeting in two or three sentences. Parents may need to hear a message more than once, so a summary is useful.

Follow-up: If a parent makes a request, I write it down immediately following the conference. I follow up and get back to parents in a timely manner. Prompt follow-up builds credibility and goodwill with parents. If anything remotely controversial was said, I report this to appropriate school personnel the following day.

124. How can I communicate honestly with parents?

It's important to be both diplomatic and honest when communicating with parents. You'll gain valuable insight into a student from his parents, because parents know their child best. While you're an educational specialist and know more about child development and teaching groups, parents are specialists when it comes to their child.

Warmth and friendliness: To establish rapport, greet parents with a handshake and invite them to sit next to you at a table, rather than across a desk. If you teach younger students, have adult-size chairs for parents. Practice active listening, maintain eye contact, and nod appropriately. I don't take notes in front of parents because I don't want to make them anxious. Instead, I jot down what I want to remember as soon as parents leave.

Tolerance and trust: It takes time for a teacher to build credibility and trust with parents. You'll meet diverse parents and families. Remain open and tolerant. Remind yourself that it's your job to teach, not to set parents straight.

Honesty: At the same time, tell parents the truth about their child. Chances are parents will hear only part of the truth, but with a consistent message over time, they will view their child more clearly. You'll know when parents are ready to hear more because they'll ask for your advice.

Here are more ideas about communicating with parents.

E-mail: The beauty of e-mail is you have a few minutes to consider what a parent has said before responding, so you're less likely to misspeak. E-mail is especially effective for quick communication, like setting up an appointment for a parent-teacher conference. Don't use e-mail to discuss specifics about a child's behavior or rebut a parent's position. E-mail is not for in-depth communication because, as a public employee, anything you write is a matter of public record. Don't write anything you wouldn't want to appear on the front page of your local newspaper.

Notes: When a parent sends a note to school, it's advisable to respond with a short note the same day. Make your note brief and to the point. Don't sound defensive, but do suggest an appointment if an issue warrants it. It's tempting to sit on a note for a day or two, but you can likely defuse a situation if you respond quickly. As with e-mail, be careful with word choice and tone. For your own protection, keep copies of notes you receive and send to parents. I keep a folder near my door for parent notes.

Phone calls: Encourage parents to call a school secretary to set up an appointment before or after school or during your planning time. Return phone calls within 24 hours. As with e-mail and notes, save controversial issues for face-to-face conferences.

Scheduled parent conferences: Schedule 30-minute conferences with parents in November and April. (For high-need students, I meet with parents more frequently throughout the year.) I have created graphic organizers for my conferences. My summary sheet contains recent assessment results, daily and homework grades, and my observations about a student's work habits and social and emotional growth.

At the beginning of a conference, I first ask parents if they have any concerns or questions. I want to hear what's on their minds so we can deal with those issues first and move on. Then I discuss pertinent data because it keeps me focused and objective. I give parents a copy of my summary sheet. They follow along as we talk and have the summary sheet to take home. Throughout the conference, I ask parents if they have questions. Along with a summary sheet I have:

- current samples of their child's work
- parenting articles
- math manipulatives (number lines, hundred charts, flash cards, etc.)
- suggested reading lists for children

Impromptu conferences in a hallway: Teaching is probably the only profession where a client walks in and demands an immediate appointment. An anxious or upset parent may drop by before school expecting to speak with you immediately. This is not in your best interest because you aren't prepared and may be drawn into an argument. Do not meet with parents when you are unprepared and under pressure to meet. You could say, "I can see you want to discuss this issue. Right now I'm helping my students start their day. I'd be happy to speak with you about this issue later today after school or tomorrow morning at 8:00 A.M."

This response may cause a parent to see the inappropriateness of his actions.

125. What can I do about an angry parent?

When a parent is angry, it's difficult to remain rational, accept their criticism, and take it in stride. Take a step back, breathe deeply, and remind yourself it's not all about you. Try to empathize and look at it from a parent's perspective.

There are logical reasons why a parent might be frustrated, particularly if his child is in trouble at school. Not all parents are equally skilled or even-tempered.

A child who is out of control at school is likely out of control at home, on the baseball field, etc. He may have learned to scream or throw tantrums from his parents. A student with symptoms of ADHD or anxiety at school shows similar symptoms at home and in the community. Both ADHD and anxiety have genetic as well as environmental components. As trained professionals, we are with students during the school day, but imagine what life is like for an untrained, anxious parent who lives with a willful, undisciplined child.

The best way to handle an angry parent is to make an appointment to sit down with him and listen to what's on his mind. Don't engage in an impromptu hallway conference. If you fear for your safety or just feel uneasy, ask a colleague, preferably a principal or school psychologist, to be present to support you and confirm what is said. Especially if other school personnel will be present, have an in-house, pre-meeting strategy session.

Be well-prepared with work samples, assessment results, and notes. Plan what you will say in advance. Focus on the facts and keep your feelings under control. Maintain a professional demeanor. If a parent starts to yell, immediately ask him to stop. If he doesn't stop, leave the meeting. Do not tolerate verbal abuse.

126. A parent accused me of raising my voice. How should I respond?

First, were you yelling? If you didn't raise your voice, try taking the following steps:

- Request a conference with this parent.
- Ask your principal to join your conference and plan to meet in her office.
- Prepare for the meeting with written notes.
- Have a pre-meeting to discuss strategy.
- Maintain a professional demeanor during the meeting.

If you were actually yelling:

- Apologize to the student and his parents.
- Inform your principal and union representative.
- Analyze why this incident occurred to ensure you don't repeat it.

127. How can I involve parent volunteers?

Here are several of many ways to involve parents in your classroom and school. Be sure to thank and formally recognize volunteers. Consider an annual Volunteer Appreciation Day.

Share special talents and interests: At Back-to-School Night, ask parents to write down interests or talents they'd like to share. Then schedule parent visits so that once every two to three weeks, a parent drops by to share. I've had parent visitors who are writers, soldiers, glass blowers, and farmers; all share their hobbies and interests.

Supervise centers: There are times when an extra pairs of adult hands are incredibly helpful. If you have learning centers, you may recruit parents or grandparents who are willing to come in a few hours a week to assist. Set up a regular schedule and publish it in your weekly newsletter.

Participate in Careers Day: Children, especially younger students, love to have parents visit to talk about what they do. Parent participation gives you insight into parent-child relationships and families.

Organize an enrichment program: You may have an existing enrichment program or want to start one. Parents in our school receive an annual arts grant that they use to plan and provide a school-wide arts enrichment program. In another after-school program, a parent volunteer and I lead a Chess Club.

Read aloud/tell stories: There are parents who love to read aloud. Grandparents might tell stories or share their childhood experiences.

Assist in computer lab: Extra adults come in handy in a computer lab.

Chaperone field trips and parties: In your school it may be permissible for parents to provide field trip transportation. Check with your administrator about your school policy. Traditionally, parents have assisted at class parties.

Assist with fund raisers and community service projects: Planning a bake sale or other fund raiser? There are parents who will bake for you and others who will sell baked goods.

Help in other ways: Parents can shelve books in a library, answer a phone in a busy office, assist a school nurse, and supervise on a playground or in a cafeteria. Think creatively about how to involve parents in your school.

128. What can I do about overinvolved parents?

In the past, a healthy tension existed between parents, who wanted to protect their children, and teachers, who wanted students to grow toward independence. Recently there has been a shift toward hyper-vigilance, over-protection, and even intrusiveness on the part of some parents.

There are a number of reasons for this change. Our fast-paced life feeds feelings of anxiety. Parents have limited time with their children and want to do their best. Fear inspired by September 11th may trouble parents. Violence at schools around the country has also affected parents. Today's parents may be unsure of their parenting skills due to lack of time spent with their own parents.

We may be more patient if we understand parents are motivated by love for their children as well as by fear. We care about their children, too, so we are in basic agreement with parents. Consider the following in working with parents:

Raise awareness: We need to be kind and clear in explaining policies and expectations to students and parents. Use school and class newsletters and PTO meetings to clarify expectations. Here are some examples of points to cover:

- Parents of young students may not be aware that carrying a second grader's backpack down a hall or hanging up his coat for him is too much.
- They may not know that interrupting a lesson or intruding at the beginning of a school day is inappropriate.
- Have protocols for parent-teacher conference appointments, drop-off and dismissal procedures, and homework help, to ease parental anxiety.

Set boundaries: While it's important for teachers to be responsive and available to parents, set appropriate boundaries. At our school, we ask parents to wait in our front hall to greet their children, rather than stand outside a classroom door. Similarly, set boundaries about e-mails, telephone calls, appointments, homework help, and notes/home-school communication. Discuss your ideas with colleagues and think through policies before Parent Night so you can explain your preferences to parents at the beginning of the school year.

Make homework independent: We can help parents let go if we structure homework so students can complete assignments independently. Ask parents to have children complete homework in a quiet place away from the kitchen, preferably at a desk. What you can do to help:

- Keep assignments short, simple, and manageable for students.
- Explain homework directions to students during the school day.
- Write a homework directions cover sheet so students can check off homework as they complete it.
- For upper-elementary and middle school students, use agenda notebooks to record homework assignments.
- Give students tools, such as hundred charts and number lines, for home use.
- Include information about the homework online.

Teach independence: Students need explicit instruction about independence with opportunities to practice at school. If you have independent, silent reading or an independent work time, this is a good time to teach what independence means.

Begin the year with structure and predictability. Give clear directions and answer questions prior to independent activities. As students mature, gradually release responsibility to them. Finally, encourage students to help one another become independent.

129. How can I have a successful Parent Night?

I have a packet I put together for Parent Night, which includes:

- my academic expectations
- curriculum overview and list of textbooks
- class rules
- discipline policy
- homework policy
- class weekly schedule
- how to reach me by e-mail and phone

If parents can't be at Parent Night, I send home their packet the following day. In addition to a packet, I have a sign-up sheet for fall parent-teacher conferences. Most parents sign up at Parent Night so I only have to make a few phone calls to schedule conferences.

In addition to bulletin boards, which display student work, students' book boxes and folders for each subject are arranged on their desktops. Each student has written his parents a short note welcoming them and asking them to look for three specific things in our classroom. There are blank sticky notes on each desk, and I encourage parents to write notes back to their children. Students love receiving notes, and a few save their notes all year. I write notes to students whose parents can't attend so everyone is included.

Parent Night has a warm, friendly tone. Imagine yourself welcoming guests to your home. First I briefly introduce myself. Then I point out things I hope they'll look at while they're visiting and ask them to leave a note for their child on his desk. Although I do talk about the curriculum for a few minutes, I spend considerable time discussing homework problems. Because I want parents to leave feeling satisfied, I repeatedly ask if they have questions.

Believe it or not, some parents are anxious about coming to school. They may have had negative school experiences growing up or perhaps English is not their first language. Whatever the reason, your warm greeting and beautiful, well-organized classroom will impress them positively.

One More Question

130. What's the most important job that teachers perform?

The most important job that teachers perform is to teach students to think. Due to the rapid pace of change, those of us teaching young children now have no notion what the world will be like in 20 years.

Our best hope for their future is to teach students to think and make school a community of thinkers. Every year I have second graders who have no concept of the life of the mind. By age 7, they have learned that school is about completing worksheets and getting correct answers. They are unaware there might be something more. However, by the end of second grade, these students can:

- argue a point and defend it with evidence from a story
- generate multiple strategies when solving math problems
- consider the feelings of others and include, rather than bully
- talk about their thinking

They have been transformed by their own thoughts. As part of a community of learners, they have awakened to what education is really about, deep thought. The following are some of the ways I teach students to think:

Higher-level thinking: Thinking beyond literal, concrete thought is encouraged in reading, writing, and discussion. Teaching cause-effect, drawing conclusions, and making inferences is just the tip of the iceberg. Students can parrot the terms, but to be internalized, higher-level thinking must be presented in meaningful contexts.

Logical thinking: Logical thinking is crucial for an understanding of math. Math is not just numbers; it is a way of thinking. Logical thinking, taught through math and games of logic, like chess, can be mastered by both girls and boys.

Creative thinking: Spending time in creative, imaginative thought is part of childhood. Children need opportunities for their imaginations to roam and find expression in play, art, music and movement. Students need puppets, costumes, Reader's Theater, skits, role-play, poetry, instrumental music, and songs/rhymes. Artistic and creative expression is not a frill; it is a human need. Creative thinking is the antithesis of test prep.

Divergent thinking: Students need to think broadly and expansively. I encourage divergent thinking when I accept multiple responses, probe using follow-up questions, and brainstorm ideas and solutions.

Convergent thinking: Bringing together facts and ideas under one umbrella, seeing connections, and analyzing situations are aspects of convergent thinking. I guide students to engage in convergent thinking as they do research in science and social studies.

Strategic thinking: Learning to plan, organize, consider options, and make good choices are all parts of strategic thinking. Successful adults are strong strategic thinkers.

Socially aware thinking: All students in a school community bring their own talents, skills, strengths, and weaknesses. Every child deserves to find acceptance and inclusion at school. Children of different races, ethnicities, religions, abilities, and genders have a right to be respected as valued community members. Community service projects and outreach to the wider community are also part of socially aware thinking.

Metacognition: "What were you thinking? Let's write down your thinking." That is what I say as I teach metacognition: thinking about thinking.